Dedicated to Jay W. Jensen friend and benefactor whose foresight made this exhibition and publication possible, to Professor Michael D. Coe mentor and scholar whose passion for ancient Mesoamerican art is legendary, and to our ancient American ancestors whose cultural legacy we hold in trust.

The Jaguar's Spots:
Ancient Mesoamerican Art from the Lowe Art Museum, University of Miami

By Traci Ardren

Contributors:
Julie K. Wesp
Gretel Rodríguez
Erica Sefton
Gabrielle Vail

Spanish Translation by:
TransPerfect Translations

Published on the occasion of the exhibition, *The Jaguar's Spots: Ancient Mesoamerican Art from the Lowe Art Museum*, University of Miami, June 26, 2010 through October 31, 2010.

Organized by Traci Ardren, Ph.D.

©2010 The Lowe Art Museum, University of Miami. No part of this publication may be reprinted or reproduced in any form, by any means, electronic or mechanical, including photocopying, or by any storage or retrieval system, without the written permission of the Lowe Art Museum, University of Miami, Coral Gables, Florida 33124.

Funding for the exhibition and catalog was made possible through the Jay W. Jensen and John W. and Thelma S. Jensen Endowment. Additional programmatic support is provided through the Department of Cultural Affairs, the Miami-Dade Mayor and Board of County Commissioners, support from the City of Coral Gables, Beaux Arts, Friends of Art, and the general membership of the Lowe Art Museum.

Library of Congress Control Number: 2010929883
ISBN: 978-0-9788213-4-3

Designed by Chris Rogers, *Yazi*
Photography by Tim McAfee
Illustrations by Mallory Fenn
Edited by Leslie Sternlieb
Printed by Dynacolor Graphics, Miami, Florida

Notes:
In dimensions, height precedes width and depth; all measurements are in inches. BCE (before the common era) and CE (common era) are used in place of BC and AD.

COVER:
Funerary Urn, Maya (Highlands (K'iche), Guatemala)
ca. 700-900 CE, Ceramic, 18 $^{3}/_{8}$ x 17 $^{3}/_{4}$ x 17 $^{1}/_{4}$"
Gift of Mr. and Mrs. Robert Stoetzer, 91.0376

BACK COVER:
Stamp, Maya (Guatemala)
ca. 600-900 CE, Ceramic, 3 x 2 $^{5}/_{8}$ x 1 $^{1}/_{2}$"
Gift of The Institute of Maya Studies, 80.0024

Table of Contents

Map:	Ancient Cultures of Mesoamerica	
Chapter 1:	Preface and Acknowledgements / Prefacio y agradecimientos BRIAN A. DURSUM	1
Chapter 2:	Introduction / Introducción TRACI ARDREN	4
Chapter 3:	The Lord of the Night: Jaguar Iconography in the Ancient Art of Mexico and Central America / El señor de la noche: iconografía del jaguar en el arte antiguo de México y América Central TRACI ARDREN	10
Chapter 4:	Maintaining the Cosmos: Myth and Ritual in Maya Painted Vessels / El mantenimiento del cosmos: mitos y rituales en las vasijas pintadas de la cultura maya GABRIELLE VAIL	16
Chapter 5:	Conversing with the Gods: Royal Maya Rituals Carved in Stone / Conversando con los dioses: rituales de la realeza maya tallados en piedra GABRIELLE VAIL	22
Chapter 6:	Performing the Creation of the World on the Miami Vase / Representando de la creación del mundo en el Jarrón de Miami TRACI ARDREN & GABRIELLE VAIL	28
Chapter 7:	Divine Beings and Oaxacan Funerary Urns in the Collection of the Lowe Art Museum / Seres divinos y urnas funerarias de Oaxaca en la colección del Museo de Arte Lowe JULIE K. WESP	34
Chapter 8:	Marine Life in the Art of Ancient Parita Bay, Panama / Vida marina en el arte antiguo de la bahía de Parita, Panamá ERICA SEFTON	38
Chapter 9:	Chicomecoatl, the Aztec Maize Goddess / Chicomecóatl, la diosa azteca del maíz GRETEL RODRÍGUEZ	42
Catalog	TRACI ARDREN Olmec Maya Veracruz & Oaxaca Central Mexico West Mexico Costa Rica & Panama	48
Staff		156
References		157
Contributors		162

CHAPTER 1:
Preface and Acknowledgments

I have been associated with the Lowe Art Museum at the University of Miami for thirty-six years in a number of roles, most recently as director. Throughout these years I have witnessed the growth and maturation of the Lowe's pre-Columbian, now Ancient American, collection. The collection now numbers more than three thousand objects. Over the years there have been a number of exhibitions that highlighted aspects of the art of the earliest indigenous peoples in the hemisphere that came to be called the Americas. In the early years of the Lowe these exhibitions were largely drawn from private collections in Miami and from other parts of the country.

In 1990, the Lowe organized the first exhibition drawn entirely from its permanent collection, *Before Discovery: Artistic Development in the Americas Before the Arrival of Columbus*. The catalog for the exhibition successfully documented the collection at that time. Produced in Spanish and English, the catalog was distrib-

CAPITULO 1:
Prefacio y agradecimientos

He estado asociado al Museo de Arte Lowe de la Universidad de Miami durante 36 años a través de diferentes funciones, más recientemente como director del museo. Durante todos estos años he sido testigo del crecimiento y la maduración de la colección precolombina del Lowe, ahora conocida como la colección de América Antigua. Esta colección ya incluye más de tres mil piezas. En el transcurso de los años, se han realizado varias exhibiciones dedicadas a destacar diversos aspectos del arte de los primeros aborígenes que habitaron el continente que más tarde se conoció como América. En los primeros años de vida del Lowe, estas exhibiciones en gran medida mostraban colecciones privadas de Miami y otros lugares del país.

En el año 1990, el Museo Lowe organizó la primera exhibición compuesta en su totalidad por su colección permanente, con el título *Before Discovery: Artistic Development in the Americas Before the Arrival of Columbus* (Antes del descubrimiento: el desarrollo artístico de América antes de la llegada de Colón). El catálogo de la

uted widely in the hemisphere. The exhibition also traveled throughout the United States and was an important step toward the museum's development of a major resource for ancient American art in the South Florida community.

In 1996, the Lowe dedicated the Jay W. Jensen, John W. and Thelma S. Jensen Wing to permanently house this important collection. Along with the dedication of the new space, Jay W. Jensen pledged $1.2 million to help fund programming for the collection. The current exhibition, *The Jaguar's Spots: Ancient Mesoamerican Art from the Lowe Art Museum, University of Miami*, is the first exhibition at the Lowe to focus entirely on the indigenous art of the peoples that occupied that part of the Americas. This region includes the eight modern nation-states of Mexico, Guatemala, Honduras, El Salvador, Nicaragua, Belize, Costa Rica, and Panama. These national boundaries, however, do not directly correspond with the cultural boundaries of the ancient American world. Maya artifacts, for example, have been found in Mexico, Guatemala, El Salvador, and Honduras. The regional influence of the Olmec, who occupied an area along the Gulf coast of Mexico, remains the subject of continuing scholarly debate.

This exhibition and accompanying catalog are intended to provide the novice and scholar with an overview of the arts and culture of the region, from the Olmec to the Aztec, as viewed through the permanent collection at the Lowe. Some of the pieces have been exhibited and documented before, but many are gifts from generous donors in the years following the 1990 exhibition and catalog and will be seen for the first time in the context of the Lowe's collection.

I would like to extend my appreciation to all our donors who have made this collection, exhibition, and catalog a reality. I would especially like to thank Dr. Traci Ardren, who, together

---

exhibición documentaba de excelente manera toda la colección existente en ese momento, estaba redactado en inglés y español, y se distribuyó ampliamente en todo el hemisferio. La exhibición también recorrió todo el territorio de Estados Unidos y representó un importante avance en la consolidación del museo como uno de los principales centros de arte de la América antigua en la comunidad del Sur de la Florida.

En 1996, el Lowe asignó el pabellón Jay W. Jensen, John W. and Thelma S. Jensen para alojar de forma permanente esta importante colección. Además de la asignación de este nuevo espacio, Jay W. Jensen comprometió $1.2 millones de dólares para ayudar a financiar programas para esta colección. La exhibición actual, denominada *The Jaguar's Spots: Ancient Mesoamerican Art from the Lowe Art Museum, University of Miami* (Las manchas del jaguar: arte antiguo mesoamericano del Museo de Arte Lowe, Universidad de Miami), es la primera exhibición del museo dedicada exclusivamente al arte aborigen de los habitantes de esa región de América, que en la actualidad comprende a los países de México, Guatemala, Honduras, El Salvador, Nicaragua, Belice, Costa Rica y Panamá. Sin embargo, las actuales fronteras de estos países no corresponden a las fronteras culturales de la América antigua. Por ejemplo, se han encontrado artefactos de la cultura maya en México, Guatemala, El Salvador y Honduras. La influencia regional de los olmecas, que ocuparon la zona situada a lo largo de la costa mexicana del Golfo, sigue siendo objeto de debate académico.

Esta exhibición y el catálogo que la acompaña procuran ofrecer a los aficionados y expertos una visión general del arte y la cultura de la región, desde los olmecas a los aztecas, a través de la colección permanente del Museo Lowe. Si bien algunas de estas piezas se han exhibido y documentado con anterioridad, muchas han sido obsequiadas por generosos donadores con posterioridad a la exhibición y al catálogo de 1990, y serán vistas por primera vez como parte de la colección del museo.

with her students, has worked diligently over the past three years to help us achieve this important milestone.

Support for the exhibition and catalogue was made possible through the Jay W. Jensen and John W. and Thelma S. Jensen Endowment. Additional programmatic support is provided through the Department of Cultural Affairs, the Miami-Dade Mayor and Board of County Commissioners, support from the City of Coral Gables, Beaux Arts, Friends of Art, and the general membership of the Lowe Art Museum.

Brian A. Dursum
Director and Chief Curator

Deseo expresar mi agradecimiento a todos nuestros donantes, quienes han permitido que la colección, la exhibición y el catálogo sean una realidad. Me gustaría agradecer especialmente a la Dra. Traci Ardren, quien, junto con sus estudiantes, trabajó arduamente durante los últimos tres años para ayudarnos a lograr este importante hito.

La exhibición y el catálogo fueron posibles gracias al apoyo de la Fundación Jay W. Jensen and John W. and Thelma S. Jensen. También se recibió apoyo programático a través del Departamento de Asuntos Culturales, el alcalde de Miami-Dade y la Junta de Comisionados del Condado, la Ciudad de Coral Gables, Beaux Arts, Friends of Art y todos los miembros del Museo de Arte Lowe.

Brian A. Dursum
Director y Curador Jefe

CHAPTER 2:
Introduction

Traci Ardren

When I was asked by museum director Brian Dursum to curate an exhibition of the best and most significant pre-Columbian art from the permanent collection of the Lowe Art Museum, I was understandably thrilled. Although a regional museum, the Lowe has a large and outstanding collection of almost one thousand objects of ancient art from Mexico and Central America. From my first days as an undergraduate, my academic passion has been the art and other symbolic representations of the New World pre-Hispanic cultures. I still have a small scrap of paper with the scrawled phrase, "how art communicates the biggest ideas of our lives," written down as a kind of touchstone during a moment of inspiration early in graduate school, when I was bombarded by new ideas and directions for research. During most of my childhood, my father worked at the John and Mable Ringling Museum of Art, and my mother worked in the theater. I was transported, time and again, to places of profound emotion and contemplation through art. When I was introduced to the an-

---

CAPITULO 2:
Introducción

Traci Ardren

Cuando Brian Dursum, director del museo, me solicitó que fuese la curadora de la exhibición de las mejores y más significativas piezas del arte precolombino pertenecientes a la colección del Museo de Arte Lowe, me embargó una lógica emoción. Si bien es un museo regional, el Lowe cuenta con una enorme y destacada colección de casi mil piezas de arte antiguo provenientes de México y América Central. Desde mis primeros días de estudiante en la universidad, he sido una apasionada estudiosa del arte y otros tipos de representaciones simbólicas propias de las culturas que poblaron el Nuevo Mundo antes de la llegada de los europeos. Todavía conservo una hoja de papel con la frase casi imposible de leer, "cómo comunica el arte las más grandes ideas de nuestras vidas", escrita como una especie de lema en un momento de inspiración al comenzar mis estudios, cuando me bombardeaban las nuevas ideas y corrientes de investigación. Durante la mayor parte de mi infancia, mi padre trabajó en el Museo de Arte John and Mable Ringling, y mi madre, en el teatro. Una y otra vez, fui transportada a lugares de profunda emoción y contemplación a través del arte. Cuando conocí

cient art of the Americas, I felt I had discovered a secret world of magic and deep, deep power.

Of course I was soon to discover that this beautiful and complex corpus was hardly my secret. Beginning in the nineteenth century, Western eyes have turned with fascination to the ancient art of the New World, and scholarship on this material continues to be extremely lively. During the Colonial period, citizens of Mexico City were drawn to Aztec sculptures that were discovered accidently in the course of an urban life lived upon the barely concealed remains of an ancient capital. And well before European contact, the Aztec royalty collected Olmec antiquities and other heirlooms, in part due to the tremendous beauty and intensity of this art. A century of research has shown that masterpieces of art were a cultural priority for the ancient peoples of Mesoamerica, the area from Mexico through Panama, and not just in the advanced states of central Mexico and the Maya area, but from the earliest appearance of social complexity. Figurines appear in this region as early as the Formative period, ca. 2000 BCE, and only five hundred years later, masterpieces of stone and jade were created in the Olmec area, such as the jade celt (2005.29.6, p50), included in this exhibition. Over the next three thousand years, from 1500 BCE to the arrival of Hernán Cortez at the Aztec capital of Tenochtitlan in 1519, many regional traditions developed, each with its own visual language, yet united by certain core values.

The pre-Columbian art of Mexico through Panama is intimately tied to the natural world, and its animals, plants, and geography provided a pervasive metaphor for the indigenous social values of this region. As in the animal world, the peoples of the ancient Americas recognized hierarchies of power, and they naturalized such hierarchies through analogy to the most powerful creatures of the tropics such as jaguars and monkeys. Rulers and gods were often represented as half human-half animal (80.0125, p80), in order to convey their innate authority

---

el arte antiguo del continente americano, sentí que había descubierto un mundo secreto de magia y total y absoluto poder.

Desde luego, pronto descubrí que este corpus de belleza y complejidad estaba lejos de ser un secreto de mi exclusividad. A partir del siglo XIX, los ojos de Occidente comenzaron a observar con fascinación el arte antiguo del Nuevo Mundo y, hasta hoy, la investigación de este material sigue transmitiendo un total entusiasmo. Durante el período colonial, los habitantes de la ciudad de México quedaron cautivados con las esculturas aztecas que se descubrieron de forma accidental e irrumpieron en la vida urbana que transcurría sobre los restos apenas ocultos de una antigua capital. Asimismo, mucho antes de entrar en contacto con Europa, la realeza azteca coleccionaba antigüedades y otras reliquias de la cultura olmeca, en parte debido a la increíble belleza e intensidad de ese arte. Después de un siglo de investigación, se ha demostrado que las obras de arte eran una prioridad cultural para los antiguos habitantes de Mesoamérica, la región que abarca desde México hasta Panamá, y no sólo a partir de los estados más desarrollados de México central y la región maya, sino también desde el más temprano advenimiento de la complejidad social. Las primeras estatuillas aparecieron en esta región ya en el período Formativo, aproximadamente 2,000 años antes de Cristo, y sólo 500 años después, en la región olmeca, se crearon obras maestras de jade y piedra, como la azuela de jade (2005.29.6, p50) incluida en esta exhibición. En los siguientes tres mil años, desde 1500 a. de C. hasta la llegada de Hernán Cortés a la capital azteca de Tenochtitlán en 1519, se desarrollaron numerosas tradiciones regionales, cada una con su propio lenguaje visual, pero a la vez unificadas por determinados valores centrales.

El arte precolombino de la zona de México a Panamá está íntimamente ligado al mundo natural, y sus animales, plantas y geografía proporcionaron una metáfora de gran significado para expresar los valores sociales de los indígenas de esta región. Al igual que en el mundo animal, los habitantes de la América antigua reconocían jerarquías de poder y las naturalizaban por me-

over the majority of the population. The intricacies of the plant world, such as the presence of female and male flowers on the same corn plant or the role of insects in pollination, were likewise an inspiration for ancient American artists. The Maize Deity was portrayed with female and male costume elements, and various sacred foods, such as the squash and crab (2008.39.14, p118 and 89.0081, p152), appear often in loving portraiture. Most of us are aware that the massive pyramids of the region are architectural echoes of the mountains and volcanoes believed by many cultures of the region to be the homeland of humans. Summit temples, represented in miniature in the exhibition (91.0010, p125 and 2007.4.17, p120), corresponded to the caves that snake through the mountains and provide a portal to the Underworld. Thus, throughout the region, individuality was often subsumed to a meta-narrative of naturalized power; seasonal cycles were relied upon to explain and contain the inevitability of change; and human dependence upon natural resources was fetishized in both comic and disturbing ways (91.0376, p79 and 86.0037, p97).

The title for this exhibition, *The Jaguar's Spots: Ancient Mesoamerican Art from the Lowe Art Museum*, was meant to draw a connection between the unique artworks on view and the distinctive markings of this powerful creature. There are many images of jaguars in the collection, from the majestic images of rulers wearing jaguar pelts (89.0080, p94) to the whimsical ceramic ocarina in the form of a two-headed cat (94.0014.09, p135), discussed in more detail in chapter 3. But jaguars are more than beautiful subject matter; they were master metaphors for authority and might. One example of this is the Order of the Jaguar, one of the two major Aztec military orders (along with the Order of the Eagle), so named because of the role a jaguar played in the creation of our current world, or what the Aztecs called the Fifth Sun. Like all Mesoamerican peoples, the Aztecs believed the world had been created and destroyed many

---

dio de analogías con las criaturas más poderosas de los trópicos, como el jaguar y el mono. Los gobernantes y los dioses con frecuencia eran representados como criaturas mitad humanas, mitad animales (80.0125, p50), con el fin de transmitir su autoridad innata sobre la mayoría de la población. Del mismo modo, las complejidades del mundo vegetal, como la existencia de flores femeninas y masculinas en una misma planta de maíz o el papel de los insectos en la polinización, eran una poderosa fuente de inspiración para los artistas de la América antigua. La deidad del maíz era representada con elementos masculinos y femeninos en su vestuario, y diversos alimentos sagrados, como la calabaza y el cangrejo (2008.39.14, p118 y 89.0081, p152), con frecuencia aparecían en retratos de índole amorosa. Casi todos sabemos que las macizas pirámides de la región son un reflejo arquitectónico de las montañas y los volcanes que, según la creencia de muchas culturas de la región, eran el lugar de origen del ser humano. Los templos más importantes, representados en miniatura en la exhibición (91.0010, p125 y 2007.4.17, p120), correspondían a las cuevas que serpenteaban a través de las montañas y ofrecían un portal al inframundo. Por lo tanto, en toda la región, la individualidad a menudo estaba subordinada a una metanarrativa del poder naturalizado. Los ciclos estacionales se utilizaban para explicar y contener la inevitabilidad del cambio, y se hacía un fetiche de la dependencia del hombre respecto de los recursos naturales, en forma cómica pero también perturbadora (91.0376, p79 y 86.0037, p97).

El título de la exhibición, *The Jaguar's Spots: Ancient Mesoamerican Art from the Lowe Art Museum* (Las manchas del jaguar: arte mesoamericano antiguo) procura establecer una conexión entre las inigualables piezas de arte que se exhiben y las manchas que caracterizan a esa poderosa criatura animal. Existen muchas representaciones de jaguares en la colección, desde las majestuosas imágenes de gobernantes vistiendo pieles de jaguar (89.0080, p94) a la enigmática ocarina de cerámica con forma de felino de dos cabezas (94.0014.09, p135), cuyas características se analizan con mayor profundidad en el capítulo 3. Sin embargo, el jaguar no

times. When it was time to create the Fifth Sun, the world in which we live today, the gods gathered in darkness at the ancient city of Teotihuacan to select one amongst them to be the new sun. The vain Tecuciztecatl stepped forward but was unable to throw himself onto the sacrificial pyre. The gods asked the old god Nanahuatzin, humble and covered in sores, to sacrifice himself. Without hesitation, Nanahuatzin threw himself onto the fire, and his animal-companion spirit, the eagle, rose blackened from the flames. Embarrassed by his elder, Tecuciztecatl jumped onto the smoldering fire, and his animal-companion spirit, the jaguar, emerged smudged where small spots of his pelt burned away. The eagle was associated with the daytime sun, and the jaguar with the night, and their valor was commemorated in the two military orders. Like the jaguar, the art of ancient Mesoamerica is primordial and courageous. Each object carries a unique message about how an individual artist living many years ago understood the emotions and experiences of their lives. It is our lucky privilege to try and puzzle out those messages today.

Modern Kaqchikel Maya artist Paula Nicho Cúmez, an oil painter who expresses strong emotions about the natural world in her art, echoes the values of interdependence seen in the objects selected for *The Jaguar's Spots*:

"I remember when I was young they would bring us to the mountains and we would yell in the forest and you could hear the echo, and so I would ask, 'Why does the echo return?' As an adult, I said to myself, 'I want to make an artwork in which I visually demonstrate the echo of the mountains.' I relate this to the cosmo-vision of our Mayan ancestors whose philosophy is that everything contains life: water, trees, mountains, and nature. In my painting, the mountains had laughing faces as they played the marimbas. This was my way of showing that mountains are alive" (Staikidis 2006:55).

I am pleased to have the opportunity to share

---

era sólo un símbolo de belleza, sino que también era una metáfora central de autoridad y poder. Un ejemplo de esto es la Orden del Jaguar, una de las dos principales órdenes militares de los aztecas (junto con la Orden del Águila), que debía su nombre al papel representado por el jaguar en la creación del mundo, o lo que los aztecas llamaban "el Quinto Sol". Como todos los pueblos mesoamericanos, los aztecas creían que el mundo había sido creado y destruido muchas veces. Cuando llegó el momento de crear el Quinto Sol, que es el mundo en el que vivimos, los dioses se reunieron rodeados por la oscuridad en la antigua ciudad de Teotihuacán para seleccionar al que sería el nuevo sol. El arrogante Tecuciztecatl se adelantó pero no pudo arrojarse a la pira de sacrificio. Los dioses entonces le pidieron al viejo dios Nanahuatzin, humilde y con el cuerpo cubierto de llagas, que se sacrificase. Sin dudar un segundo, Nanahuatzin se arrojó a la hoguera y el águila, el espíritu animal que lo acompañaba, surgió ennegrecido de las llamas. Avergonzado, Tecuciztecatl se arrojó a las brasas y su espíritu animal, el jaguar, emergió de las llamas con rastros de tizne donde pequeños trozos de su pelaje se habían quemado. El águila se relacionó con el sol y el jaguar con la noche, y el valor de ambos fue conmemorado en dos órdenes militares. Al igual que el jaguar, el arte de la antigua Mesoamérica es primordial y valeroso. Cada pieza transmite un mensaje único sobre la forma en que un artista que vivió muchos años atrás comprendía las emociones y las experiencias de la vida. Hoy, tenemos el afortunado privilegio de intentar descifrar esos mensajes.

Paula Nicho Cúmez, la artista moderna de origen maya kaqchikel quien a través de la pintura al óleo expresa en su arte profundas emociones sobre el mundo natural, rememora los valores de interdependencia que se observan en los objetos seleccionados para la colección *The Jaguar's Spots*:

Recuerdo que en mi niñez, nos llevaban al monte y gritábamos en el bosque y se podía escuchar el eco, entonces yo me preguntaba, "¿Por qué regresa el eco?". Ya siendo una mujer adulta, me dije a mí misma: "Quiero hacer una pieza de arte

175 of the most important objects from the permanent collection of pre-Columbian art at the Lowe Art Museum. The Lowe began collecting in this area in the 1950s, and one of its earliest acquisitions, the Chicomecoatl sculpture (56.003.000, p110), remains a key part of the collection and is featured in chapter 9. Through the generosity of many donors the collection has grown to include strengths in Costa Rican pottery, Aztec, and Olmec sculpture, and, with the addition of the Miami Vase (2009.26, p84) in honor of this exhibition, Classic Maya pottery. The second director of the Lowe from 1956-1964, C. Clay Aldridge, was a Harvard-trained anthropologist and is credited with the vision to build a strong Native American collection in South Florida. In addition to early purchases of pre-Columbian art, he secured both the Lothrop collection of Guatemalan textiles and the Barton collection of Southwestern textiles, pottery, and kachinas. Since 1971, The Institute for Maya Studies (IMS) has been an active presence in Miami, and we are grateful for a number of objects donated by IMS members to the museum collection over the past thirty years.

The art of ancient Mexico and Central America speaks to all audiences. Even if one is not an expert in the detailed iconography of Zapotec funerary urns or Maya hieroglyphic texts, the energy and passion of this artwork is easily accessible. I was pleased to include undergraduate students in some of the preliminary research for this exhibition, as part of two courses I teach at the University of Miami. Students in a museum internship course spent time conducting an inventory of this large collection and doing background research on every object. Students in Ancient Civilizations of Mesoamerica visited the Lowe's Mesoamerican gallery, chose objects on which to write detailed research reports, and examined the objects under the supervision of museum staff. Many of the interpretations generated by these students have been incorporated into the exhibition catalog and I am grateful for their participation. Both my classroom teach-

---

en la que pueda mostrar visualmente el eco de las montañas". Esto lo relaciono con la cosmovisión de nuestros ancestros mayas, cuya filosofía es que todo tiene vida: el agua, los árboles, las montañas y la naturaleza. En mis pinturas, las montañas sonríen mientras tocan las marimbas. Ésta fue mi manera de mostrar que las montañas están vivas (Staikidis 2006:55).

Me complace profundamente tener la oportunidad de compartir 175 de las más importantes piezas de la colección permanente de arte precolombino del Museo de Arte Lowe. El Lowe comenzó a crear una colección sobre el tema en la década de 1950, y una de sus primeras adquisiciones, la escultura de Chicomecoatl (56.003.000, p110), sigue siendo una parte clave de la colección y se presenta en el capítulo 9. Gracias a la generosidad de muchos donadores, la colección ha crecido hasta incluir objetos fundamentales de la alfarería de Costa Rica, esculturas aztecas y olmecas y, con la adición del Jarrón de Miami (2009.26, p84) en honor a esta exhibición, alfarería clásica maya. C. Clay Aldridge, segundo director del Museo Lowe entre 1956 y 1964, fue un antropólogo de Harvard reconocido por su visión de crear una sólida colección de arte nativo americano en el Sur de la Florida. Además de realizar las primeras adquisiciones de arte precolombino, Aldridge consiguió la colección Lothrop de tejidos guatemaltecos y la colección Barton de tejidos, cerámicas y cachinas de la región sudoeste. Desde 1971, el Instituto de Estudios Mayas (Institute for Maya Studies, IMS) mantiene una presencia activa en Miami, y agradecemos los numerosos objetos donados por los miembros de IMS a la colección del museo en los últimos 30 años.

El arte antiguo de México y América Central es para todo tipo de público. No hace falta ser un experto en la detallada iconografía de las urnas funerarias zapotecas o en los jeroglíficos mayas, porque la energía y la pasión de estas obras se transmite con mucha facilidad. Me sentí muy complacida al incluir estudiantes universitarios en algunas de las investigaciones preliminares para esta exhibición, como parte de los dos cursos que dicto en la Universidad de Miami. Los estudiantes de pasantía dedicaron su tiempo a

ing and the process of designing and curating this exhibition have been enriched by finding avenues through which learning and research could go hand in hand. I especially wish to thank Gretel Rodríguez and Erica Sefton, my curatorial assistants for this exhibition, with whom collaborating has been a true pleasure. I also acknowledge the generosity of many colleagues who have commented on these objects in the course of preparation for the opening of *The Jaguar's Spots*, including Alejandra Alonso, Roland Betancourt, Jeffrey Blomster, John B. Carlson, Ximena Chávez, Michael D. Coe, Mallory Fenn, Stanley Guenter, Christine Hernandez, Angel Huitzilin, Bryan R. Just, Barbara and Justin Kerr, Tim Knowlton, Rex Koontz, Matthew Looper, Martha Macri, Matthew H. Robb, Adam T. Sellen, Karl Taube and Marc Zender. Finally, this exhibit would not have succeeded without the talented support of the Lowe Art Museum staff, especially Kara Schneiderman, Assistant Director for Collections, and Dr. Brian Dursum, Director and Chief Curator.

For further information:

Miller, Mary Ellen. 2001. *The Art of Mesoamerica: From Olmec to Aztec*. Thames and Hudson, New York.

Staikidis, Kryssi. 2006. Where Lived Experiences Reside in Art Education: A Painting and Pedagogical Collaboration with Paula Nicho Cúmez. *Visual Culture and Gender* 1:45-62.

Taube, Karl. 1993. *Aztec and Maya Myths*. University of Texas Press, Austin.

---

realizar un inventario de esta gran colección y a investigar y obtener información sobre cada pieza. Los estudiantes de la curso de Civilizaciones Antiguas de Mesoamérica visitaron la galería de Mesoamérica del Lowe, eligieron objetos sobre los que escribieron detallados informes de investigación y examinaron las piezas bajo la supervisión del personal del museo. Muchas de las interpretaciones generadas por los estudiantes fueron incorporadas al catálogo de la exhibición, y les agradezco profundamente su participación. Tanto mis actividades de enseñanza como el proceso de diseñar y curar esta exhibición se enriquecieron al encontrar nuevos caminos en los que el aprendizaje y la investigación fueran de la mano. Quisiera agradecer especialmente a Gretel Rodríguez y a Erica Sefton, mis asistentes de curaduría en esta exhibición, con quienes ha sido un verdadero placer colaborar. También deseo agradecer la generosidad de muchos colegas que realizaron observaciones acerca de estas piezas durante la preparación para la apertura de la exhibición *The Jaguar's Spots*, entre ellos a Alejandra Alonso, Roland Betancourt, Jeffrey Blomster, John B. Carlson, Ximena Chávez, Michael D. Coe, Mallory Fenn, Stanley Guenter, Christine Hernandez, Angel Huitzilin, Bryan R. Just, Barbara y Justin Kerr, Tim Knowlton, Rex Koontz, Matthew Looper, Martha Macri, Matthew H. Robb, Adam T. Sellen, Karl Taube y Marc Zender. Finalmente, esta exhibición no habría sido posible sin el talentoso apoyo de todos los trabajadores del Museo de Arte Lowe, en especial de Kara Schneiderman, Directora Asistente de Colecciones, y del Dr. Brian Dursum, Director y Curador Principal.

Material de consulta para obtener más información:

Miller, Mary Ellen. 2001. *The Art of Mesoamerica: From Olmec to Aztec*. Thames and Hudson, New York.

Staikidis, Kryssi. 2006. Where Lived Experiences Reside in Art Education: A Painting and Pedagogical Collaboration with Paula Nicho Cúmez. *Visual Culture and Gender* 1:45-62.

Taube, Karl. 1993. *Aztec and Maya Myths*. University of Texas Press, Austin.

CHAPTER 3:

The Lord of the Night: Jaguar Iconography in the Ancient Art of Mexico and Central America

Traci Ardren

Within today's Western scientific community, jaguars remain a poorly understood and understudied large cat, but the ancient peoples who lived in Mexico and Central America prior to European contact were very familiar with the habits of the largest and most powerful land predator of the region. Olmec and Maya art are both known for their striking images of this fierce and beautiful creature, and indigenous people from southern Mexico all the way through to Panama chose to portray the jaguar in their artistic creations. One of the themes explored in this exhibition is the close interconnection between the ancient peoples of Central America and the natural world in which they lived—a largely tropical world, of rainforests and mountains, rich in animal life, and embraced by the sea. Scholarship has shown that the cultures represented in this exhibition did not exist in idyllic harmony with their natural environment—the urban centers of central Mexico and the Maya area show clear evidence of environmental degradation—yet they also had

CAPITULO 3:

El señor de la noche: iconografía del jaguar en el arte antiguo de México y América Central

Traci Ardren

A pesar de que para la comunidad científica occidental el jaguar sigue siendo sólo un gran felino poco estudiado y comprendido, los pueblos que antiguamente habitaron la zona de México y América Central antes de la llegada de los europeos estaban muy familiarizados con los hábitos del más grande y poderoso depredador terrestre de la región. El arte olmeca y el arte maya se caracterizan por las impactantes imágenes de esta feroz y bella criatura, y los aborígenes que habitaron desde el sur de México hasta Panamá elegían al jaguar para representarlo en sus creaciones artísticas. Uno de los temas analizados en esta exhibición es la estrecha interrelación que existió entre los antiguos pueblos de América Central y el mundo natural en el que vivían, un entorno tropical pleno de selvas y montañas con una fauna rica y variada, abrazado por el mar. Las investigaciones han demostrado que las culturas representadas en esta exhibición no convivían en idílica armonía con el entorno natural, y los centros urbanos del área central de México y la región maya muestran claras evidencias de degradación ambiental. Sin embargo, también

a respect for the ambient world that far exceeds our own today and were better able to balance human and environmental needs. Objects were selected that span a period of more than two thousand years, from the earliest signs of social complexity in the Olmec area to the height of cosmopolitan urbanism in the Aztec capital, but throughout this massive span of time the powerful creatures of the natural world remained a primary metaphor in artistic expression and the communication of social values.

The jaguar, *Panthera onca*, is the third-largest cat in the world and the most powerful predator of the New World tropics. Jaguars live solitary lives deep in the forest and are primarily nocturnal, becoming active just after sunset. An adult female jaguar will want up to thirty square miles for her range, with an adult male occupying up to fifty square miles, and territory is aggressively defended by each adult male. Jaguars are famous for their ability to swim and catch waterborne prey, and they are the only large cats to live in swamps and wetlands, as well as deep jungle and mountain scrub. During the time when the art in this exhibition was produced, jaguars roamed from the southwestern United States through Mexico and Central America and deep into South America. Jaguars love the water, and will often bathe or play in rivers and springs, stopping only to snack on fish or turtles. Although one of the very few animals capable of killing a human in the tropical New World, jaguars are shy and documented reports of attacks against humans are exceedingly rare.

The admiration for jaguars shown in the art of the ancient indigenous peoples of Central America was most likely inspired not by fear of actual attack, but rather on the mutual respect and accommodation that scientists think characterizes the normal (non-industrialized) interactions of humans and jaguars throughout the region. They point out that jaguars have the full spectrum of forest animal life available for food, and that humans are the least com-

---

existía un respeto por el entorno muy superior al que mostramos actualmente y un mejor equilibrio entre las necesidades del hombre y de la naturaleza. Los objetos seleccionados abarcan un período de más de dos mil años, desde las primeras señales de complejidad social en el área olmeca hasta la cumbre del urbanismo cosmopolita de la capital azteca. No obstante, durante este enorme período de tiempo, las poderosas criaturas del mundo natural siempre fueron una metáfora primaria en la expresión artística y la comunicación de los valores sociales.

El jaguar *(Panthera onca)* es el tercer felino de mayor tamaño del mundo y el depredador más poderoso de los trópicos del Nuevo Mundo. Los jaguares llevan una vida solitaria en la profundidad de la selva, y son animales principalmente nocturnos cuyas actividades comienzan después del crepúsculo. Una hembra adulta necesita ocupar una extensión de hasta 30 millas cuadradas (casi 78 km2) y un macho ocupa hasta 50 millas cuadradas (casi 130 km2), y cada macho defiende agresivamente su territorio. Los jaguares son famosos por su habilidad para nadar y atrapar presas acuáticas, y son los únicos grandes felinos que pueden vivir en terrenos pantanosos y zonas húmedas además de las selvas y los montes. En los tiempos en que se crearon las piezas de arte de esta exhibición, los jaguares habitaban la región que hoy abarca desde el sudoeste de Estados Unidos, México y América Central, y gran parte de América del Sur. A los jaguares les encanta el agua, y con frecuencia se bañan en ríos o manantiales, donde sólo se detienen para apresar peces o tortugas. Si bien es uno de los pocos animales de la zona tropical del Nuevo Mundo capaz de matar a un ser humano, el jaguar es tímido y son muy excepcionales los informes documentados sobre ataques al hombre.

Es muy probable que la admiración por el jaguar reflejada en el arte de los pueblos antiguos de América Central no se inspirase en el miedo a un ataque sino en la adaptación y el respeto mutuo que, en opinión de los científicos, caracterizaban a las interacciones normales (no industrializadas)

mon animal of the forest. In many ways, the art displayed in *The Jaguar's Spots* confirms this finding—from the pumice jaguar figurine from Panama (90.0126.76, p154) to the Maya ceramic vase with a jaguar-head decoration (94.0054.02, p75)—the art of precontact indigenous Mexico and Central America emphasizes the majesty of this impressive cat rather than its fearsome or ferocious aspect. A palpable sense of awe is conveyed for the cat who loves water, the elusive lord of the night, the territorial loner.

Olmec culture had one of the most complex conceptualizations of the jaguar and is famous for art that depicts an anthropomorphized jaguar cub, or what some have called a "were-jaguar." One of the most visually impressive objects in this exhibition is a jade celt (2005.29.6, p50), an excellent example of this artistic tradition that formed one of the core components of how leadership and authority were expressed. Precious masterpieces like this object were painstakingly crafted by master artisans to be used in rituals where a local leader conveyed his supernatural abilities to the populace through a mystical association with the powers of the jaguar. The identification of the jaguar with leaders persisted in Mesoamerica for thousands of years, and in the Classic Maya period the jaguar was both a spiritual companion for certain dynastic rulers and a totem of royal power as seen in the use of jaguar pelts on kingly thrones or dress, depicted on vases 86.0199, p87 and 89.0080, p94. Royals also wore jade pendants in the form of jaguar claws such as 83.0031-32, p65, and 2003.63.80, p67 to demonstrate their association with one of the most dangerous aspects of this great cat.

Respect and even awe for the jaguar is also communicated through the various myths and stories of ancient Mesoamerica in which deities take on jaguar characteristics. On the Classic Maya polychrome bowl 85.0071, p60, we can see a series of head-variant glyphs, and of the eight deities portrayed on the bowl, two take jaguar form. One is the Jaguar Paddler, an assistant to

---

entre el hombre y el jaguar en toda la región. Estas interacciones indican que mientras los jaguares tenían a su disposición todo el espectro de fauna silvestre de la región para alimentarse, el hombre era el animal menos común de la selva. En muchos sentidos, las piezas de arte exhibidas en *The Jaguar's Spots* confirman estos hallazgos, desde la figurilla de jaguar en piedra pómez proveniente de Panamá (90.0126.76, p154) hasta la vasija de cerámica maya con decoración de cabeza de jaguar (94.0054.02, p75): el arte de los pueblos de México y América Central antes de la llegada de los europeos destaca la majestuosidad de este impresionante felino y no el miedo que inspira ni su aspecto feroz. Se transmite un palpable sentimiento de veneración por el felino que ama el agua, el esquivo señor de la noche, el solitario en su territorio.

La cultura olmeca presentaba una de las más complejas conceptualizaciones del jaguar y es famosa por su arte que representa a un jaguar antropomorfo, o lo que algunos llaman el "hombre-jaguar". Una de las piezas de la exhibición de mayor impresión visual es la azuela de jade (2005.29.6, p50), un excelente ejemplo de esta tradición artística que fue uno de los componentes centrales de la forma en que se expresaban la autoridad y el liderazgo. Preciosas piezas de arte como este objeto eran esmeradamente creadas por artesanos maestros para ser utilizadas en rituales en los que un líder local mostraba sus habilidades sobrenaturales a la población mediante una asociación mística con los poderes del jaguar. La identificación del jaguar con el líder persistió en Mesoamérica durante miles de años, y en el período maya clásico el jaguar fue tanto un acompañante espiritual de determinadas dinastías gobernantes como un emblema del poder real, tal como puede observarse en el uso de pieles de jaguar en tronos o ropajes de la realeza, según las representaciones de las vasijas 86.0199, p87 y 89.0080, p94. Los miembros de la realeza también usaban pendientes de jade con forma de garras de jaguar, como se puede observar en las piezas 83.0031-32, p65 y 2003.63.80, p67, para demostrar su vínculo con uno de los aspectos más peligrosos de este felino.

the Maize Deity on his path of rebirth, and the other is the famous Hero Twin Xbalanque, who is always distinguishable by the black jaguar spots on his face and body (see chapter 4 for more on this vase). Xbalanque is often shown with his twin brother and their probable father the Maize Deity, as seen on the Miami Vase (2009.26, p84), where Xbalanque is dressed as a hunter in a ritualized reenactment of the rebirth of the Maize Deity. Look for his jaguar spots and you will find him. A fearsome aspect of jaguar power is conveyed by the Postclassic Maya censor (80.0125, p80), a clay vase designed to hold burning resin incense. The figure is part woman, part jaguar, and as Gabrielle Vail notes in chapter 4, may portray the female creator/destroyer deity Chak Chel in her wild aspect as the uncontrolled forces of the jungle.

In the ancient art of Costa Rica and Panama we see similar ideas regarding the jaguar as an embodiment of power and status. The beautiful high-status pottery of the late Guanacaste region was used for feasting and ceremonies by the high-ranking leaders of this area. The lovely bowl with the head of a jaguar (86.0076, p145) even carries within its legs small clay balls meant to rattle as it was delivered to a ruler, perhaps as a signal that the vessel itself was alive. Another object in the exhibition from Costa Rica, the jaguar effigy jar (72.016.009, p132), was most likely made as an offering to accompany the burial of a high-status chief. The stone mace head in the form of a jaguar (88.0008, p138), originally mounted on a wooden handle, was also probably made to accompany an elaborate internment, as close examination reveals it was never used in battle. Mace heads were indicators of rank, but also possibly of clan affiliation. Among the Bribri people of Costa Rica, only people of the jaguar or monkey clans were eligible to become chiefs. Twin jaguars are depicted in the gold pendant (2007.52.20, p137), which may have been worn into battle to impress enemies as well as used in ceremonies to capture the power of the sun. Thus again we see

---

El respeto, e incluso la veneración por el jaguar también se transmiten a través de diversos mitos y relatos de la antigua Mesoamérica en los que las deidades adoptan características del jaguar. En el bol policromático del período clásico maya (pieza 85.0071, p60), podemos observar una serie de glifos de variantes de cabeza y, de las ocho deidades representadas, dos tienen forma de jaguar. Una es el Remero Jaguar, que ayudaba a la deidad del maíz en su camino al renacimiento, y la otra es el famoso Héroe Gemelo Xbalanqué, que siempre puede distinguirse por las manchas negras de jaguar en su rostro y su cuerpo (véase el capítulo 4 para obtener más información sobre esta vasija). Con frecuencia, Xbalanqué es representado con su hermano gemelo y su probable padre, el Dios del Maíz, tal como puede observarse en el Jarrón de Miami (2009.26, p84), en el que Xbalanqué aparece vestido como cazador en una reconstrucción ritualizada del renacimiento de la deidad del maíz. Si buscamos las manchas del jaguar, podremos identificarlo. Un aspecto atemorizante del poder del jaguar es representado por el incensario del período preclásico maya (80.0125, p80), una vasija de arcilla diseñada para quemar incienso. La figura es en parte femenina y en parte jaguar, y tal como observa Gabrielle Vail en el capítulo 4, es posible que represente a la deidad femenina creadora/destructora Chak Chel en su aspecto salvaje de fuerza descontrolada de la jungla.

En el arte antiguo de Costa Rica y Panamá observamos ideas similares sobre el jaguar como la encarnación del poder y del estatus. Las hermosas piezas de alfarería de alto estatus correspondientes a la región de Guanacaste eran utilizadas para fiestas y ceremonias por los líderes de más alta jerarquía de esta zona. El maravilloso bol con cabeza de jaguar (86.0076, p145) incluso contiene en sus patas pequeñas esferas de arcilla para generar un sonido al entregar el bol a un líder, quizás como señal de que la vasija misma tenía vida propia. Otro objeto de la exhibición proveniente de Costa Rica, la jarra con efigie de jaguar (72.016.009, p132), muy probablemente fue creada como una ofrenda para acompañar a un gobernante de alto nivel en su entierro.

the unique energy and intensity of the largest cat in the New World employed as a metaphor for supernatural authority and control.

Sadly, today jaguars are greatly threatened by human encroachment. Although they were placed on the U.S. endangered species list in 1997, there was never an effort to recover much of their native habitat. The last known wild jaguar within the United States was tragically killed in a bungled snaring incident in 2009. The following year the Center for Biological Diversity won a legal battle to protect jaguar habitat in the United States, and the Obama administration pledged to develop a recovery plan and protect essential habitat for the great cat. Protection efforts in Central America have been more successful, where the first jaguar preserve was established in 1990 at the Cockscomb Basin Wildlife Sanctuary in Belize. The 128,000-acre reserve was established as a result of the pioneering research on jaguars conducted by Alan Rabinowitz and chronicled in his popular memoir *Jaguar: One Man's Struggle to Establish the World's First Jaguar Preserve*. Jaguars are also protected in reserves within Mexico, Brazil, and Peru. One lesson we can learn from the diverse and beautiful art displayed in *The Jaguar's Spots* is that humans have long looked to powerful animals for lessons and inspiration—a quest that requires mutual respect and accommodation in order to yield answers.

For further information:
Kubler, George. 1986. *Pre-Columbian Art of Mexico and Central America*. Yale University Art Gallery, New Haven.

Rabinowitz, Alan. 2000. *Jaguar: One Man's Struggle to Establish the World's First Jaguar Preserve*. Island Press, Washington D.C.

También es probable que la cabeza de maza de piedra con forma de jaguar (88.0008, p138), originalmente montada sobre una empuñadura de madera, se haya fabricado para acompañar un elaborado enterramiento, ya que un minucioso examen muestra que nunca se utilizó en batalla. Las cabezas de mazas indicaban una determinada jerarquía, pero también es posible que indicaran la pertenencia a un clan. En los pueblos bribri de Costa Rica, sólo los miembros de los clanes del jaguar o del mono podían ser elegidos jefes. Pueden observarse jaguares gemelos en el pendiente de oro (2007.52.20, p137), que posiblemente se utilizó en combate para impresionar a los enemigos y también en ceremonias para capturar el poder del sol. Esto nos demuestra una vez más la forma en que la energía y la intensidad del más grande felino del Nuevo Mundo se utilizaban como una metáfora del control y la autoridad sobrenatural.

Lamentablemente, en la actualidad se cierne una peligrosa amenaza sobre los jaguares a causa de la usurpación humana de sus territorios. Si bien en el año 1997 fueron incluidos en la lista de especies en peligro de Estados Unidos, nunca se realizaron esfuerzos por recuperar una gran parte de su hábitat natural. El último jaguar salvaje de Estados Unidos del que se hayan tenido noticias murió trágicamente en un incidente de caza con trampas en el año 2009. Al año siguiente, el Centro de Diversidad Biológica (Center for Biological Diversity) ganó una batalla legal para proteger el hábitat del jaguar en Estados Unidos, y el gobierno del presidente Obama se comprometió a desarrollar un plan de recuperación y a proteger el hábitat esencial de este gran felino. En América Central, los esfuerzos proteccionistas han tenido más éxito, ya que en 1990 se estableció la primera reserva natural de jaguares en Cockscomb Basin Wildlife Sanctuary, en Belice. Esta reserva de 128,000 acres (casi 520 km2) se creó como resultado de las investigaciones pioneras sobre los jaguares realizadas por Alan Rabinowitz y narradas en sus famosas crónicas *Jaguar: One Man's Struggle to Establish the World's First Jaguar Preserve* (Jaguar: la lucha de un hombre para establecer la primera reserva

de jaguares del mundo). Los jaguares también son protegidos en reservas de México, Brasil y Perú. Una de las lecciones que podemos aprender de la diversidad y la belleza del arte exhibido en *The Jaguar's Spots* es que el ser humano siempre ha buscado sabiduría e inspiración en los animales poderosos, y esta búsqueda requiere de adaptación y respeto mutuo para poder arrojar respuestas.

Material de consulta para obtener más información:

Kubler, George. 1986. *Pre-Columbian Art of Mexico and Central America.* Yale University Art Gallery.

Rabinowitz, Alan. 2000. *Jaguar: One Man's Struggle to Establish the World's First Jaguar Preserve.* Island Press.

CHAPTER 4:

Maintaining the Cosmos: Myth and Ritual in Maya Painted Vessels

Gabrielle Vail

For the pre-Hispanic Maya, events from the mythic past were believed to play a key role in the present, as were the characters who populated the ancient stories—figures like the Maize Deity, who journeyed to the Underworld and was sacrificed, but who, like the maize plant, undergoes rebirth; his sons the Hero Twins; and the rain and lightning gods, known as Chahk and K'awiil, who freed maize from its hiding place deep within a mountain so it could be used by the creator goddess to fashion humans. These deities, or humans who take on their attributes, are featured on many Classic period Maya ceramics. Other vessels highlight the lives of the Maya elite, presenting an in-depth view of life within the royal Maya court.

One of the functions of the royal court was to host ceremonial and dynastic events that included the use of elaborately painted or incised Maya vessels. These can take many forms, the most common being bowls and plates that would have held food, and cylindrical vases used

---

CAPITULO 4:

El mantenimiento del cosmos: mitos y rituales en las vasijas pintadas de la cultura maya

Gabrielle Vail

En la cultura maya prehispánica, se creía que los eventos del pasado mítico influían decisivamente en el presente, al igual que los personajes que poblaban los antiguos relatos, como la deidad del maíz, que viajó al inframundo y fue sacrificada pero, al igual que la planta del maíz, volvió a renacer; sus hijos, los héroes gemelos, y los dioses de la lluvia y el rayo, conocidos como Chahk y K'awiil, quienes descubrieron el maíz que estaba oculto dentro de la montaña y permitieron que la diosa creadora lo utilizase para dar forma a los seres humanos. Estas deidades, o los hombres que adoptaban sus atributos, son representados en muchas piezas de cerámica del período clásico maya. Otras vasijas destacan la vida de la élite maya y presentan una profunda mirada sobre el acontecer diario en la corte real.

Una de las funciones de la corte real consistía en organizar ceremonias y eventos dinásticos que incluían el uso de vasijas pintadas o labradas de forma elaborada. Estas piezas adquieren diferentes formas, y las más comunes son los tazones o fuentes que posiblemente contenían alimentos,

for ceremonial drinks, most commonly in the form of a chocolate beverage known as cacao (Maya *kakaw*). These and other elaborately decorated polychrome vessels were manufactured for special occasions such as feasts and were given in gift exchanges. Feasting was—and continues to be—an integral part of Maya ceremonies.

The hieroglyphic texts and images on Maya vessels serve a narrative function, illustrating the inseparable relationship between politics, myth, and ritual among the Classic period Maya elite. Painted scenes often feature an indoor setting such as a royal palace and may show the ruler seated on a bench or throne covered by a jaguar pelt, as shown on the Miami Vase, (2009.26, p84) in this exhibition. Jaguars were revered throughout Mesoamerica for their fierceness and valor, and rulers frequently identified themselves with this creature, either by wearing a jaguar pelt as part of their costume or by adopting the word for jaguar *(bahlam)* as part of their names.

The Maya recognized several different jaguar deities, including the nighttime sun (called the Jaguar God of the Underworld) and the Hero Twin Xbalanque, known in pre-Hispanic texts as Yax Bahlam or "First Jaguar." He and his twin Hunajpu (or Hun Ajaw) were the sons of the Maize Deity and played a role in Maya mythology similar to that of twins in many Native American traditions—freeing the world of monsters, establishing order and balance, and preparing the earth for the creation of humans. Following their adventures, they rose into the sky to become the sun and the moon.

Jaguars are a common theme of the Maya polychrome vessels in the exhibition. At times, they are depicted in their naturalistic form, such as the example modeled on the handle of the lid of vessel (86.0188, p88), and in other instances take on human characteristics, as shown on bowl (81.0224, p90), where the jaguar wears a scarf around its neck. On bowls (86.0199, p87) and (89.0080, p94), warriors are represented wear-

---

y los vasos cilíndricos utilizados para bebidas ceremoniales que casi siempre consistían en una bebida de chocolate llamada cacao (*kakaw* en maya). Éstas y otras vasijas policromáticas de elaborada decoración se fabricaban para ocasiones especiales, como banquetes y fiestas, y se intercambiaban a manera de obsequios. Los banquetes eran, y siguen siendo, una parte integral de las ceremonias mayas.

Los jeroglíficos e imágenes que aparecen en las vasijas mayas cumplen una función narrativa e ilustran la inseparable relación entre la política, los mitos y los rituales en la élite maya durante el período clásico. Las escenas pintadas suelen representar espacios interiores, como el palacio real, y pueden mostrar al gobernante sentado en un banco o un trono y cubierto con pieles de jaguar, tal como se observa en el Jarrón de Miami (2009.26, p84) que se incluye en esta exhibición. Los jaguares eran reverenciados en toda Mesoamérica por su ferocidad y su valor, y con frecuencia los líderes se identificaban con esta criatura, ya sea mediante el uso de pieles de jaguar como parte de sus ropajes o bien adoptando la palabra que denominaba al jaguar *(bahlam)* como parte de sus nombres.

Los mayas reconocían diferentes deidades jaguares, entre las que se incluyen al sol de la noche (llamado el Dios Jaguar del Inframundo) y al Héroe Gemelo Xbalanqué, que en los textos prehispánicos aparece como Yax Bahlam o "Primer Jaguar". Xbalanqué y su hermano gemelo Hunajpu (o Hun Ajaw) eran los hijos del Dios del Maíz, y en la mitología maya representaban un papel similar al de los gemelos de muchas tradiciones nativas de América: liberaban al mundo de los monstruos, establecían el orden y el equilibrio y preparaban la tierra para la creación de los seres humanos. Después de vivir sus aventuras, se elevaron al firmamento y se convirtieron en el sol y la luna.

Los jaguares son un tema que se repite en las vasijas policromáticas mayas que forman parte de la exhibición. Algunas veces eran representados en su forma más natural, como en el ejem-

ing jaguar costumes, which on occasion may include a full jaguar pelt. A figurine of a female deity with jaguar characteristics, (80.0125, p80), reveals that women as well as men were associated with this fierce creature. Indeed, the female creator deity Chak Chel is sometimes shown with clawed hands and feet to indicate her connection with this animal. It is thought that the jaguar may have been one of her animal alter egos.

Jaguar deities are also featured on bowl (85.0071, p60), which includes the portrait glyphs of eight deities who play seminal roles in Classic Maya mythic narratives. Included are the Hero Twins (p60, A1 and B1), as well as a pair of gods known as Jaguar Paddler and Stingray Paddler (at C1 and D1), who were responsible for paddling a canoe containing the Maize Deity from the Underworld to the place of his rebirth; this is typically depicted as his emergence from the cracked carapace of a turtle. Metaphorically, this can be related to the sprouting of the maize from seeds planted within the earth.

Among the pre-Hispanic Maya and some contemporary Maya cultures, individuals are identified with particular animals (their co-essences), as revealed to them in dreams. This is also true of Maya deities. The Maize Deity is closely associated with the quetzal, a bird found in the highland regions that was prized for its long, beautiful tail feathers, which were frequently worn by Maya nobles as part of their headdresses or capes, as seen on vessel (93.0043.03, p83). Because of his connection with rebirth, the Maize Deity served as a model for many Maya lords, who emulated his youthful appearance (discussed in detail in chapter 6) and adopted his symbols of fertility, including maize foliage and quetzal plumes.

Several of the vessels in the exhibition include hieroglyphic texts, which add considerably to our understanding of the activities and relationships expressed graphically on Maya ceramics. Texts may be in one of two forms—a formulaic text known as the Primary Standard Sequence

---

plo modelado en el asa de la tapa de la vasija (86.0188, p88), mientras que en otras instancias adoptaban características humanas, tal como puede observarse en el bol (81.0224, p90), en el que el jaguar lleva una bufanda alrededor de su cuello. En los tazones (86.0199, p87) y (89.0080, p94), aparecen guerreros que usan trajes de jaguar, lo cuales en ocasiones podían incluir toda la piel del animal. La figurilla de la deidad femenina con características del jaguar (pieza 80.0125, p80) muestra que las mujeres también eran vinculadas con esta feroz criatura. De hecho, la diosa creadora Chak Chel en ocasiones es representada con garras en las manos y los pies para indicar su conexión con la fiera, y se cree que el jaguar puede haber sido una de sus personalidades animales.

Las deidades jaguares también están representadas en el bol (85.0071, p60), que incluye glifos de retrato de ocho deidades que jugaban un papel primordial en los relatos míticos clásicos de los mayas. Aquí se incluyen los Héroes Gemelos (p60, A1 y B1) y también a un par de dioses

conocidos como el Remero Jaguar y el Remero Mantarraya (en C1 y D1), que eran los que conducían la canoa en la que el Dios del Maíz viajaba desde el inframundo al lugar donde renacía. Habitualmente, esto se representa mostrando cómo surge del caparazón roto de una tortuga. Metafóricamente, este mito puede relacionarse con el florecimiento del maíz a partir de las semillas sembradas en la tierra.

En la cultura maya prehispánica y algunas culturas mayas contemporáneas los individuos se identifican con determinados animales (su coesencia), la cual se revela en sueños. Esto también se aplica a las deidades. El Dios del Maíz tiene una estrecha relación con el quetzal, un ave que habita en las zonas altas y que fue muy valorado por su cola de largas y bellas plumas, las que frecuentemente eran utilizadas por los nobles mayas como parte de sus tocados o capas, tal como puede observarse en la vasija (93.0043.03, p83). Debido a su vínculo con el renacimiento, el Dios del Maíz servía de modelo para muchos señores mayas que imitaban su apariencia juve-

(PSS), or captions to the scene pictured. PSS texts include one or more of the following: a dedicatory statement; a phrase describing the process of painting the vessel; a description of the vessel type; a description of the contents (most commonly a *kakaw* beverage); and (optionally) the name and title of the vessel's owner. Texts that are related more specifically to the vessel scene may include speech, as indicated by a scroll, such as the text appearing before the figure seated on the throne in the Miami Vase (2009.26, p84).

Bowl (86.0210, p92) is the only vessel in the exhibition with a PSS text. It differs from the standard formula in several ways (note that it is incised, rather than painted) and represents a variant form known as the Chocholá style, which archaeologists Traci Ardren and Nikolai Grube link to northern Campeche in the western part of the Yucatán Peninsula. Its text describes it as a thin-walled drinking cup (*u jay yuk'ib* at F1 and G1) of an individual described as *cholom sajal* (H1 and I1); he is also named as a *bakab* (K1). The meaning of *cholom* remains obscure, but *sajal* is a well-known title associated with subordinate lords (i.e., individuals subordinate to a named *ajaw*), and *bakab* is a title commonly used by Classic period rulers. It refers to four deities who were said to have survived the destruction of the previous world and were responsible for supporting the sky at each of the four quadrants of the present world. The unusual spelling on this vessel, as ba-(ka)-kab (the "ka" in parentheses is not pronounced but serves instead to duplicate the initial sound of the *kab* glyph), rather than ba-ka-ba, mirrors its reading as *ba(h)* "first" *kab* "world," which has been translated as "first in the world."

In Mesoamerican cosmologies, there is no clear separation between the natural and supernatural realms. In their human or animal forms, deities are expressions of forces or energies that occur in the natural world (the rain, lightning, wind, and so forth). Maya rulers and other members of

---

nil (esto se analiza en detalle en el capítulo 6) y adoptaban sus símbolos de fertilidad, entre ellos el follaje del maíz y las plumas del quetzal. Varias de las vasijas de la exhibición incluyen textos jeroglíficos, lo que resulta un valioso aporte para entender las actividades y relaciones representadas gráficamente en las cerámicas mayas. Los textos pueden tener dos formas: pueden ser textos formulistas, lo que se conoce como Secuencia Estándar Primaria (SEP), o bien leyendas al pie de la escena representada. Los textos SEP incluyen uno o más de los siguientes elementos: una dedicatoria, una frase que describe el proceso de pintar la vasija, una descripción del tipo de vasija, una descripción de su contenido (por lo general la bebida de cacao o *kakaw*), y (de forma opcional) el nombre y el título del dueño de la vasija. Los textos que se relacionan de manera más específica con la escena representada en la vasija puede incluir un discurso, indicado por una voluta, como el texto que aparece delante de la figura sentada en el trono en el Jarrón de Miami (2009.26, p84).

El tazón (86.0210, p92) es la única pieza de la exhibición con un texto SEP. Este texto se diferencia de la fórmula estándar de varias formas (es importante notar que está grabado y no pintado) y representa una variante conocida como el estilo Chocholá, que los arqueólogos Traci Ardren y Nikolai Grube relacionan con la zona norte de Campeche, en la parte occidental de la Península de Yucatán. El texto describe la pieza como un vaso para beber de paredes delgadas (*u jay yuk'ib* en F1 y G1) perteneciente a un individuo descrito como *cholom sajal* (H1, I1) y *bakab* (K1). El significado del término *cholom* sigue siendo desconocido, pero *sajal* es un título conocido que se relaciona con señores subordinados a un líder (individuos subordinados a un *ajaw*), en tanto *bakab* es un título habitualmente utilizado por los gobernantes del período clásico que hace referencia a las cuatro deidades que se decía que habían sobrevivido a la destrucción del mundo anterior y que eran responsables de sostener el firmamento en cada uno de los cuatro cuadrantes del mundo actual. La extraña ortografía que aparece en esta vasija, ba-(ka)-

the royal court took on attributes of these beings and participated in rituals in which the ancestors and deities were called forth to intervene in human affairs. It was through these rituals that the members of the royal court maintained order and balance in the world—not only for themselves, but for their subjects.

The pageantry of courtly life depicted on Classic period polychromes highlights these rituals and the roles played by different members of the court. What appear to be the most secular of events—preparations for battle or the display of tribute—were all performed with a single purpose in mind: to nurture and sustain the deities. For almost a millennium, the Preclassic and Classic period Maya were able to maintain a balanced cosmos through ritual performances such as those portrayed on the pottery and sculpture displayed in the exhibition.

For further information:

Coe, Michael, and Justin Kerr. 1998. *The Art of the Maya Scribe.* Harry N. Abrams, London.

Reents-Budet, Dorie. 1994. *Painting the Maya Universe: Royal Ceramics of the Classic Period.* Duke University Press, Chapel Hill.

---

kab (la sílaba "ka" no se pronuncia sino que duplica el sonido inicial del glifo *kab*) en lugar de ba-ka-ba, refleja las palabras *ba(h)* "primer" *kab* "mundo", que pueden interpretarse como "primero en el mundo".

En la cosmología mesoamericana, no existe una clara separación entre el reino natural y el mundo sobrenatural. En sus formas humanas o animales, las deidades son expresiones de fuerzas o energías que se manifiestan en el mundo natural (la lluvia, el rayo, el viento, etc.). Los gobernantes mayas y otros miembros de la realeza adoptaban los atributos de estos seres y participaban en rituales en los que los ancestros eran convocados para intervenir en los asuntos humanos. A través de estos rituales, los miembros de la corte real mantenían el orden y el equilibrio en el mundo, no sólo para ellos mismos sino también para sus súbditos.

La magnificencia de la vida de la realeza descrita en las piezas policromáticas del período clásico destaca estos rituales y el papel que jugaron los diferentes miembros de la corte. Los eventos que parecen ser los más seculares, como los preparativos para el combate o las muestras de tributo, se realizaban con un solo propósito en mente: preservar y sustentar a los dioses. Durante casi mil años, los períodos preclásico y clásico de la cultura maya lograron mantener el equilibrio del cosmos mediante rituales como los que se muestran en las piezas y las esculturas de esta exhibición.

Material de consulta para obtener más información:

Coe, Michael, y Justin Kerr. 1998. *The Art of the Maya Scribe.* Harry N. Abrams, London.

Reents-Budet, Dorie. 1994. *Painting the Maya Universe: Royal Ceramics of the Classic Period.* Duke University Press, Chapel Hill.

CHAPTER 5:
Conversing with the Gods: Royal Maya Rituals Carved in Stone

Gabrielle Vail

All of Maya history, according to the thousands of texts available to us, was divinely sanctioned. Few objects associated with elite Maya culture appear without hieroglyphic texts or, in their absence, iconographic elements symbolizing particular deities or forces. Texts provided a means of recording sacred messages and of contextualizing the actions of individuals within the cosmological underpinnings of the universe by linking them to the calendar and its cycles of meaning. Indeed, time itself was thought to be a manifestation of sacred forces. The ritual calendar of 260 days paired a deity representing a number between one and thirteen with a day symbolizing a particular manifestation of the physical universe (water, wind, or breath, night or darkness, maize, the earth, death, etc.). Some of these manifestations can be seen on objects in this exhibition such as the bowl (85.0071, p60), which includes portrait glyphs representing eight deities important in pre-Hispanic Maya mythology.

CAPITULO 5:
Conversando con los dioses: rituales de la realeza maya tallados en piedra

Gabrielle Vail

Toda la historia maya, segun los miles de textos disponibles, fue sancionado por las divinidades. Pocos objetos asociados con la élite de la cultura maya aparecen sin textos jeroglificos, o, en lugar de textos, presentan elementos iconograficos que simbolizan ciertas deidades o fuerzas. Los textos permitían registrar los mensajes sagrados y contextualizar las acciones de las personas dentro de los pilares cosmológicos del universo, al relacionarlos con el calendario y sus ciclos de significado. De hecho, el tiempo mismo era considerado una manifestación de las fuerzas sagradas. El calendario ritual de 260 días unía a una deidad, representada por un número entre el uno y el trece, con un día que simbolizaba una manifestación particular del universo físico (agua, viento o respiración, noche u oscuridad, maíz, tierra, muerte, etc.). Algunas de estas manifestaciones pueden observarse en algunos objetos de la exhibición, como el cuenco (85.0071, p60), que incluye glifos de retratos que representan ocho deidades importantes de la mitología maya prehispánica.

Pottery vessels, discussed in chapter 4, were one of several media used to record the myths that were central to Maya ritual and dynastic life. Mythological scenes are also portrayed in other painted contexts, including screenfold books known as codices and in murals painted on the floors, walls, and ceilings of buildings.

Scenes depicted on stone monuments, on the other hand, usually feature human subjects, although they are often shown participating in rituals that may include the presence of divine ancestors, anthropomorphic deities, or other supernaturals. These monumental sculptures, like Stela (89.0006, p78), were erected to commemorate important events in the dynastic history of particular sites, including an individual's heir-designation ceremony or accession to the status of king (*ajaw*); the display of ceremonial regalia to mark key events in the Maya calendar such as the end of the approximately twenty-year period known as the *k'atun*; rituals, including bloodletting and scattering incense, performed in honor of particular ancestors or deities; and the display of prisoners following a battle.

The stone sculptures in the exhibition feature many of these themes. Stela 89.0006, which is described as Late Classic in style (600–900 CE), has a short glyphic text (now largely eroded) that would have included the date being celebrated, a verb describing the event, and the name of the individual portrayed. Although we are missing his name, we can infer much about him based on what he is wearing, which includes an elaborate plaited headdress containing feathers from the quetzal bird and an image of the Jester God at its summit. The Jester God is an emblem of rulership that some scholars associate specifically with the Maya Maize Deity. It, together with the quetzal feathers, serves to link the figure pictured with maize agriculture, food production, and fertility. Quetzals signify times of plenty, represented by the phrase *oox wi'il*, "an abundance of food," in the Maya codices.

Las vasijas de alfarería, analizadas en el capítulo 4, fueron uno de los diversos medios utilizados para registrar los mitos que fueron fundamentales para los rituales y la vida de las dinastías mayas. Las escenas mitológicas también están representadas en otros contextos pictóricos, incluidos los libros plegables conocidos como códices y los murales pintados en los pisos, las paredes y los techos de los edificios.

Por otro lado, las escenas representadas en los monumentos de piedra, por lo general incluyen seres humanos, aunque a menudo aparecen participando en rituales que podían incluir la presencia de ancestros divinos, deidades antropomórficas u otros seres sobrenaturales. Estas esculturas monumentales, como la estela (89.0006, p78), se levantaron para conmemorar eventos importantes en la historia dinástica de ciertos sitios, incluidos, entre otros, la ceremonia de nombramiento del heredero o la toma de posesión del rey *(ajaw)*; la muestra de ropajes ceremoniales para marcar eventos claves en el calendario maya, por ejemplo, el final del período de veinte años, conocido como el *k'atun*; los rituales, como las sangrías y el esparcimiento de incienso, realizados en honor a ciertos ancestros o deidades, y la exhibición de prisioneros después de una batalla.

Las esculturas de piedra de la exhibición incluyen muchos de estos temas. La estela 89.0006, descrita como del período clásico tardío (600 a 900 d. de C.) tiene un texto glífico corto (actualmente bastante erosionado) que pudo haber incluido la fecha que se celebraba, un verbo que describía el evento y el nombre de la persona representada. Si bien nos falta el nombre, podemos inferir muchas cosas sobre esta persona en base a lo que lleva puesto: un tocado trenzado muy elaborado con plumas de quetzal y una imagen del Dios Bufón en la cresta. El Dios Bufón es un emblema de poder que muchos estudiosos asocian, principalmente, con la deidad maya del maíz. Esto, junto con las plumas de quetzal, ayuda a relacionar la figura representada con la agricultura del maíz, la producción de alimentos y la fertilidad. Los quetzales significan tiempos de

The individual depicted on the stela also wears a beaded jade necklace with a pendant, what appear to be jade wristlets, and a distinctive style of sandal similar to those worn in ritual contexts by Maya men living in highland Chiapas, Mexico, today. The event being commemorated is not entirely clear, although previous commentators have suggested that it shows the ruler letting blood from his genitals.

Bloodletting is a common theme of Classic period Maya art. The best-known examples come from a series of doorway lintels from the site of Yaxchilán, located on the Usumacinta River in Mexico. One of these shows Lady Kab'al Xook, the wife of an eighth-century ruler, pulling a stingray spine through her tongue; the resulting blood is collected on strips of paper, which will later be burned. This leads to the opening of a portal (represented by a serpent or centipede with gaping jaws) that provides a conduit to the spirit world. By this means, an ancestor or deity may be summoned to provide counsel and guidance when needed.

Bloodletting rituals are also portrayed in the Postclassic Maya codices. Page 19b of the Madrid Codex, for example, shows five deities, each connected by a rope, performing a communal bloodletting ceremony. This scene has been interpreted as the feeding of the sun (represented by a *k'in* "sun" glyph on the rope) by the blood of the gods in order to set it in motion. It highlights the importance of the gods (or of the elite, as representatives of the deities) in maintaining order in the cosmos. Other scenes that focus on bloodletting portray the human gift of blood being offered in exchange for the gods' gift of maize and other foods. For the Maya, maize is the quintessential substance: it not only forms the most significant part of their diet, but is the material out of which the gods fashioned humans.

If the figure pictured on Stela 89.0006 is indeed performing a bloodletting ritual, then it offers a parallel to scenes from the Madrid Codex in which the sacrifice of blood is matched by the

---

prosperidad, representados en los códices mayas por la frase *oox wi'il*, "abundancia de alimentos".

La persona representada en la estela también lleva un collar de jade en forma de cuentas con pendiente, brazaletes de jade y un par de sandalias de estilo característico, similares a las que usan en los rituales los hombres mayas que viven en las tierras altas de Chiapas, México, actualmente. El evento que se conmemora no está del todo claro, aunque algunos tratadistas anteriores han sugerido que lo que se muestra es al gobernante sangrando de sus genitales.

El sangramiento es un tema común en el arte del período clásico maya. Los ejemplos mejor conocidos provienen de una serie de dinteles de puertas en el sitio arqueológico de Yaxchilán, ubicado en el río Usumacinta, en México. Uno de estos muestra a la señora Kab'al Xook, esposa de un gobernante del siglo VIII, clavándose la púa de una pastinaca en la lengua; la sangre derramada se recolectaba en tiras de papel para luego quemarla. Esto conduce a la abertura de un portal (representado por una serpiente o un ciempiés con mandíbulas abiertas) que sirve de conducto para pasar al mundo espiritual. Mediante esta práctica, un ancestro o deidad puede ser llamado para que proporcione asesoramiento y orientación cuando sea necesario.

Los rituales de sangría también están representados en los códices mayas del período posclásico. La página 19b del Códice Madrid, por ejemplo, muestra a cinco deidades, cada una conectada por una cuerda, realizando una ceremonia del sangramiento comunal. Esta escena ha sido interpretada como la alimentación del sol (representada por un *k'in* glifo del "sol" en la cuerda) con sangre de los dioses para ponerlo en movimiento. Resalta la importancia de los dioses (o de la élite, como representantes de las deidades) para mantener el orden en el cosmos. Otras escenas que se centran en las sangrías, describen la ofrenda de sangre humana que se entrega a cambio de la ofrenda de los dioses de maíz y otros alimentos. Para los mayas, el maíz es el elemento por excelencia: no sólo constituye

gift of maize—an idea suggested by the Jester God image worn in the headdress of the figure portrayed on the stela.

Another offering commonly depicted in Maya art involves the scattering of incense. Although there is no accompanying image, a scattering event is described in the upper-left glyph block of the fragment from the Seibal hieroglyphic stairway in the exhibition (93.0043.04, p75). This section of text records the actions performed by K'awiil Chan K'inich, *ch'ul ajaw* (holy lord) of Dos Pilas, who celebrated this ritual at the site of Seibal on May 30, 746 (7 Etz'nab 16 Xul in the Maya calendar). According to other textual sources, Dos Pilas won a decisive victory over Seibal approximately ten years earlier.

Like many Maya rulers, K'awiil Chan K'inich was named for one of the principal Maya deities, in this case K'awiil. (Others commonly chosen include the sun god K'inich Ajaw and the rain god Chahk.) By assuming K'awiil's name, he identified himself with the powers associated with this deity, the god of lightning, who was responsible for releasing the substance of life (maize and rain) to the world of humans. Rulers on Maya monuments are frequently portrayed holding K'awiil's image, thereby linking themselves with this powerful generative deity.

Figure 1

Rollout photograph K1599 © Justin Kerr

la parte más importante de su alimentación, sino que también es el material de donde los dioses crearon a los humanos.

Si la figura representada en la estela 89.0006 está realmente realizando un ritual de sangría, entonces ofrece un paralelo con las escenas del Códice Madrid en el que el sacrificio de sangre equivale a la ofrenda del maíz, una idea sugerida por la imagen del dios Bufón que aparece en el tocado de la figura descrita en la estela.

Otra ofrenda representada a menudo en el arte maya es el esparcimiento de incienso. Si bien no hay una imagen concurrente, un evento similar se describe en el bloque de glifos superior izquierdo del fragmento de la escalinata jeroglífica de Seibal, en la exhibición (93.0043.04, p75). Esta sección de texto registra las acciones realizadas por K'awiil Chan K'inich, *ch'ul ajaw* (rey sagrado) de Dos Pilas, quien celebró este ritual en Seibal, el 30 de mayo de 746 (7 Etz'nab 16 Xul en el calendario maya). Según otras fuentes, Dos Pilas ganó una victoria decisiva sobre Seibal, aproximadamente diez años antes.

Como muchos de los gobernantes mayas, K'awiil Chan K'inich recibió su nombre en honor a una de las principales deidades mayas, en este caso K'awiil. (Otros elegidos comúnmente incluyen al

K'awiil Chan K'inich is portrayed scattering incense on another monument, Stela 1, from the nearby site of Aguateca, dated to 741, the year that he assumed the position of *ajaw* at Dos Pilas. He is shown dressed in ceremonial regalia (including a jaguar pelt skirt), with incense dropping from his open hand. This gesture mimics the "scattering" glyph seen on monument (93.0043.04, p75). Incense, like blood, was one of the substances that was burned and offered to the gods as a form of sustaining nourishment.

Another portrait of K'awiil Chan K'inich appears on a painted vessel that shows the ruler seated on a dais, receiving petitions from the two individuals facing him (figure 1). They may be identified as petitioners by the bouquets of flowers they are carrying, an offering still used in parts of the Maya area by those requesting favors. The seated figure facing K'awiil Chan K'inich is identified as a scribe by the paintbrush emerging from his turban-like headdress.

He may, in fact, be the person responsible for painting the vase, which pictures K'awiil Chan K'inich six years before his accession, according to epigraphers Simon Martin and Nikolai Grube.

Pottery scenes such as this one reflect the rich inner life of Maya courts, in contrast to the more formalized portraits depicted on carved stone monuments meant for public display. These monuments were believed to serve as manifestations of the ruler and whichever divinities were portrayed. K'awiil, as an embodiment of the power of lightning and its generative capacity, was an especially potent symbol used in Maya rituals by rulers and priests for a period of over 1500 years during which hieroglyphic texts were recorded.

---

dios del sol, K'inich Ajaw, y al dios de la lluvia, Chahk.) Al asumir el nombre de K'awiil, la persona se identifica con los poderes asociados con la deidad: el dios del relámpago que era responsable de liberar la sustancia de la vida (el maíz y la lluvia) sobre el mundo de los humanos. Los gobernantes que aparecen en los monumentos mayas, frecuentemente se representan sosteniendo la imagen de K'awiil, ligándose así a esta poderosa deidad generadora.

K'awiil Chan K'inich es representado esparciendo incienso en otro monumento, la estela 1, cerca del sitio de Aguateca, con fecha 741, el año en que asumió el título de *ajaw*, en Dos Pilas. Aparece vestido con los ropajes ceremoniales (incluida una falda de piel de jaguar), con el incienso cayendo de su mano abierta. Este ademán es similar al glifo correspondiente a "esparcir" que se puede observar en el monumento (93.0043.04, p75). El incienso, al igual que la sangre, era uno de los elementos que se quemaban y se ofrecían a manera de sustento.

Otra representación de K'awiil Chan K'inich aparece en una vasija pintada que muestra al gobernante sentado en un estrado, recibiendo las peticiones de dos personas que lo miran de frente (figura 1). Ellos pueden ser identificados como solicitantes gracias a los ramos de flores que llevan, una ofrenda que todavía se usa en ciertas partes de la región maya para solicitar favores. La figura sentada de frente a K'awiil Chan K'inich es identificada como un escriba por el pincel que sale de turbante. Es muy probable que él mismo sea la persona responsable de pintar el jarrón, que representa a K'awiil Chan K'inich seis años antes de subir al trono, según los epigrafistas Simon Martin y Nikolai Grube.

Las escenas de alfarería como ésta, reflejan la rica vida interna de las cortes mayas, en contraste con los retratos más formales representados en monumentos de piedra tallada para ser exhibidos públicamente. Se creía que estos monumentos eran manifestaciones del gobernante y de las divinidades que representaba. K'awiil, encarnación del poder del relámpago y

For further information:

Martin, Simon and Nikolai Grube. 2008. *Chronicle of the Maya Kings and Queens*. 2nd ed. Thames and Hudson, New York and London.

Taube, Karl A. 1992. *The Major Gods of Ancient Yucatan*. Studies in Pre-Columbian Art and Archaeology, No. 32. Dumbarton Oaks, Washington, DC.

---

de la procreación, fue un símbolo especialmente poderoso que se utilizó en los rituales mayas por los gobernantes y los sacerdotes durante un período de más de mil quinientos años, en el que se registraron textos jeroglíficos.

Material de consulta para obtener más información:

Martin, Simon y Nikolai Grube. 2008. *Chronicle of the Maya Kings and Queens*. 2a ed. Thames and Hudson, New York and London.

Taube, Karl A. 1992. *The Major Gods of Ancient Yucatan*. Studies in Pre-Columbian Art and Archaeology, No. 32. Dumbarton Oaks, Washington, DC.

CHAPTER 6:
Performing the Creation of the World on the Miami Vase

Traci Ardren and
Gabrielle Vail

The Miami Vase (2009.26, p84), acquired for this exhibition by the Lowe Art Museum in 2009 from a private collection in New York City (its name derives from the general convention that vases without other known provenance are named after their holding institutions), is an extraordinary example of the fine artistry exemplified in Classic Maya ceramic vases. This important acquisition is a lesser-known example of the "codex style" tradition, so named by scholar Michael D. Coe for the fine calligraphic lines of black ink on cream-colored background that resemble the written books, or codices, of the Classic Maya elite. Artists of the Classic period depicted palace and mythological scenes on large numbers of cylindrical vases that they used in elaborate feasts and presented to one another on royal visits. The codex-style vases, made in the area surrounding the ancient center of Nakbe, in modern Guatemala, are some of the most beautiful and elaborate of these masterpieces.

Codex-style vases were made in palace workshops during the late seventh and early eighth

---

CAPITULO 6:
Representando de la creación del mundo en el Jarrón de Miami

Traci Ardren and
Gabrielle Vail

El Jarrón de Miami (2009.26, p84), adquirido para esta exhibición por el Museo de Arte Lowe en 2009, y que antes pertenecía a una colección privada de la ciudad de Nueva York (su nombre se debe a la convención general que determina que las piezas sin procedencia conocida reciben el nombre de las instituciones a las que pertenecen), es un extraordinario ejemplo del elevado arte ilustrado en las piezas de cerámica del período clásico maya. Esta importante adquisición es un ejemplo menos conocido de la tradición del "estilo códice", llamado así por el académico Michael D. Coe por las finas líneas caligráficas de tinta negra dispuestas sobre un fondo de color crema que rememora los libros escritos o códices de la élite maya del período clásico. Los artistas del período clásico representaron escenas palaciegas y mitológicas en un gran número de vasos cilíndricos que se utilizaron en sofisticados banquetes y que se intercambiaban como obsequios en las visitas de la realeza. Los vasos de estilo códice, realizados en la zona que rodea el antiguo centro de Nakbe, en lo que hoy es Guatemala, son algunas de las más hermosas y elaboradas de estas piezas de arte.

century CE. Members of the royal family who were not heir to the throne were often trained as artists or scribes and spent their days creating unique art that glorified the accomplishments of their dynasty. The Miami Vase was likely the result of collaboration between a potter who formed the vessel, an artist who painted the figures upon a slipped surface, and a scribe, who added the four textual passages. The vessel may have originally been commissioned as part of the funerary assemblage of a powerful ruler or to commemorate a specific ritual accomplishment of the principal figure portrayed on the vase.

There are seven individuals visible in the rollout photograph of the Miami Vase by Justin Kerr, in what at first glance is a typical scene of sec-ondary lords visiting a king inside his palace (figure 1, K3469/K9193). Upon closer examination, however, is it clear the individuals are not normal human actors but people who have taken on the personas or identities of deities and other supernatural characters. The artist has depicted a sacred ritual within the private chambers of a king—one performed by royal occupants of the palace who were familiar with the mythological underpinnings of noble prerogative. As Gabrielle Vail explains in chapter 4, Maya history was divinely sanctioned, and the elites who ruled Maya cities were responsible for perpetuating a complicated ritual cycle based on the cosmological underpinnings of the universe.

The first three figures on the left-hand side of the composition are dressed as hunters. Hunt-

Figure 1

Rollout photograph K3469/K9193 © Justin Kerr

Los vasos de estilo códice se fabricaron en talleres palaciegos entre fines del siglo VII y principios del siglo VIII d. de C. Con frecuencia, los miembros de la familia real que no eran herederos al trono recibían educación como artistas o escribas, y dedicaban sus días a crear piezas de arte únicas que glorificaban los logros de sus dinastías. Es probable que el Jarrón de Miami sea el resultado de la colaboración entre un alfarero que moldeó la vasija, un artista que pintó las figuras en una superficie lisa y un escriba que agregó los cuatro pasajes de texto. Existe la posibilidad de que la vasija se haya encargado originalmente como parte de los objetos funerarios de un poderoso gobernante o para conmemorar un ritual específico de la figura representada en el vaso.

En la primera fotografía del Jarrón de Miami realizada por Justin Kerr pueden distinguirse siete personas, en lo que a primera vista parece una escena típica de señores de menor rango que visitaban al rey en su palacio (figura 1, K3469/K9193). Sin embargo, a través de un examen más minucioso resulta evidente que no se trata de seres humanos comunes, sino de individuos que han adoptado las personalidades o identidades de dioses y otros personajes sobrenaturales. El artista representó un ritual sagrado celebrado en las habitaciones privadas de un rey, un ritual llevado a cabo por los ocupantes de estirpe real del palacio que estaban familiarizados con los fundamentos mitológicos de las prerrogativas de la nobleza. Tal como Gabrielle Vail explica en el capítulo 4, la historia maya se apoyaba en la acción de los dioses, y las élites que gobernaban las ciudades mayas debían perpetuar un complejo ciclo ritual sobre la base de los fundamentos cosmológicos del universo.

ing was both a daily responsibility for much of the Classic population, who did not raise many domesticated animals for food, as well as a royal activity with a strong mythological linkage to the figures known as the Hero Twins, renowned as skilled hunters themselves. All three of these figures carry spears and wear elaborate animal headdresses. These animals, such as the quetzal worn by Figure 1 and the deer by Figure 3, may represent companion spirits of the men that would aid the hunters in their quest. Figures 2 and 3 are dressed as the Hero Twins—Figure 2 has markings on his face that resemble the distinctive jaguar spots of Xbalanque, and Figure 3 wears the supernatural deer headdress associated with ballplayers, hunters, and other men who perform important activities related to the mythological exploits of the Hero Twins. The ability of these twins, sons of the preeminent Maize Deity, to outwit their foes and excel at competitive tasks established the ideal of masculine behavior for royal men of the Classic period.

Figures 3 and 4 are clearly conversing, as indicated by the speech scrolls linking them to the hieroglyphic text that appears between them (text 2, p84). It says,

t'ab'ay ye?/ha'i? tu kuch

This may be translated as:

Ye? ascended/journeyed with his burden, or As for him, he [an unamed subject] ascended/journeyed on the litter.

The text may be referring to Jun Ye Nal, the name of the young Maize Deity, the first sprout that emerged from the earth. This is most likely the identity of Figure 4, who is either the Maize Deity (and father of the Hero Twins) himself, perhaps conjured by the human individuals in this palace ritual, or a human who has taken on the persona of the Maize Deity during ritual. He has a K'awiil figure emerging from the front of his headdress and a Jester God on top of his head, both symbols of royal prerogative. His head has been shaved in scribal fashion, with a fringe in front, short "sprouts" of hair on top, and a long braid down his back. This image is very similar to others of the young Maize Deity

---

Las primeras tres figuras que aparecen en el lado izquierdo de la representación están vestidas como cazadores. La caza era una responsabilidad diaria de la mayoría de la población del período clásico, quienes no criaban muchos animales domésticos para la alimentación, pero también era una actividad propia de la realeza con un profundo vínculo mitológico con figuras como los Héroes Gemelos, famosos por su habilidad como cazadores. Las tres figuras llevan lanzas y usan elaborados tocados de animales. Estos animales, como el quetzal que se observa en la figura 1 y el ciervo de la figura 3, pueden representar los espíritus acompañantes de estos hombres que ayudan a los cazadores en su búsqueda. Las figuras 2 y 3 están vestidas como los Héroes Gemelos. La figura 2 muestra marcas en su rostro que imitan las manchas del jaguar características de Xbalanqué, en tanto la figura 3 usa el tocado del ciervo que se relaciona con jugadores de pelota, cazadores y otros hombres que realizaban importantes actividades vinculadas con las hazañas mitológicas de los Héroes Gemelos. La habilidad de estos Héroes Gemelos, hijos del Dios del Maíz, para superar a sus enemigos y destacarse en competencias estableció el ideal de comportamiento masculino de los hombres de la realeza del período clásico.

Claramente, las figuras 3 y 4 están conversando, tal como lo indican las volutas que los relacionan con el texto en jeroglíficos que aparece entre ellos. En el texto se lee (texto 2, p84):

t'ab'ay ye?/ha'i? tu kuch

Esto puede traducirse como:

¿Ye? ascendieron/viajaron con su carga, o bien, dirigiéndose a un sujeto tácito: Ascendió/viajó en su litera.

El texto puede referirse a Jun Ye Nal, el nombre del Dios del Maíz en su juventud, el primer retoño que surgió de la tierra. Es muy probable que ésta sea la identidad de la figura 4, que es el Dios del Maíz (padre de los Héroes Gemelos), que quizás fue invocado por estos hombres en el ritual palaciego, o bien, un humano que adoptó la personalidad de esta deidad durante el ritual. Se observa la figura de K'awiil que emerge de la parte delantera de su tocado y al Dios Bufón sobre su cabeza, ambos símbolos de prerrogativa real. Su cabeza está afeitada al estilo de los

as scribe, especially the well-known figure on the "resurrection plate," which shows the rebirth of the Maize Deity through a crack in the turtle shell carapace of the earth. The text between Figure 3 and Figure 4 suggests that the spears the hunters bring to the ritual may assist the rebirth of the Maize Deity, perhaps by cracking open the earth like planting sticks or creating some other opening for the release of his power.

Above the young Maize Deity is the caption (text 3, p84):

to'oj? u lak? pitzil
The ballplayer's clay vessel? is paid/given in tribute.

The Hero Twins were accomplished ballplayers and one of their most famous adventures in the Underworld involved playing ball against the Lords of Death. Their father was also a ballplayer, although his adventures in the Underworld ended in his decapitation. This text suggests the Miami Vase was an offering by one or more individuals enacting the role of the Hero Twins as ballplayers in this scene. Vessels were commonly given in tribute, which is the most likely interpretation of the text caption.

To the right of Jun Ye Nal is Figure 5, a ruling king seated on his throne. The throne is covered in a jaguar pelt, owing to his royal status, and it is marked with the crossed sticks that symbolize the sky band, another indication of his power. The sky band indicates that the individual is in a celestial location, or that he possesses supernatural power. A number of elements suggest this ruler has taken on the persona of Chahk, the powerful Maya rain god. He holds an axe, used by Chahk to open the sky, and wears a Tlaloc shield of battle and a distinctive long textile headdress like the one worn at times by Chahk. His eyes are shown not as normal human eyes but with the spirals associated with supernaturals. Through his ritual tools and engagement with fellow participants, the king has achieved a deep level of contact with one of the most important gods of the Maya pantheon. Chahk was responsible for splitting the earth open so the Maize Deity could be reborn, a profound

---

escribas, con un flequillo en la frente, pequeños "brotes" de pelo en la parte superior y una larga trenza en su espalda. Esta imagen es muy similar a otras del joven Dios del Maíz como escriba, especialmente la conocida figura que aparece en el "plato de la resurrección", que muestra el renacer de la deidad a través de la grieta de un caparazón de tortuga que simboliza la tierra. El texto que aparece entre las figuras 3 y 4 sugiere que las lanzas que los cazadores traen al ritual pueden utilizarse para ayudar a renacer al Dios del Maíz, quizás abriendo una grieta en la tierra a modo de palos para plantar o creando otras aberturas para dejar salir su poder.

Sobre el Dios del Maíz puede leerse este texto (texto 3, p84):

to'oj? u lak? pitzil
La vasija de cerámica del jugador de pelota se da en forma de pago o tributo.

Los Héroes Gemelos eran destacados jugadores de pelota, y una de sus más famosas aventuras en el inframundo incluía un juego en contra de los Señores de la Muerte. Su padre también era un jugador de pelota, aunque sus aventuras en el inframundo terminaron con su decapitación. Este texto sugiere que el Jarrón de Miami era una ofrenda entregada por uno o varios hombres que representaban el rol de los Héroes Gemelos como jugadores de pelota en esta escena. Habitualmente, las vasijas se entregaban a modo de tributo, lo que resulta la interpretación más probable del texto de la escena.

A la derecha de Jun Ye Nal aparece la figura 5, un rey sentado en su trono. El trono está cubierto por pieles de jaguar debido a su condición real y aparece marcado por ramas cruzadas que simbolizan la banda celeste, otra indicación de su poder. La banda celeste indica que esta persona se encuentra en un lugar celestial o que posee poderes sobrenaturales. Diversos elementos sugieren que este gobernante ha adoptado la personalidad de Chahk, el poderoso dios maya de la lluvia. Se observa que sostiene un hacha, utilizada por Chahk para abrir los cielos, y usa un escudo de batalla de Tláloc y un característico tocado largo de tela similar al que a veces usa Chahk. Sus ojos no se muestran como los de un ser humano normal, sino con espirales relacionadas con lo sobrenatural. A través de estas herramientas

act of world creation that ensured not only the continuation of the annual rains for a fruitful agricultural cycle, but also the perpetuation of royal rule, in the form of a script which conferred authority upon new kings, who thereby modeled themselves after the Maize Deity.

The text immediately in front of the ruler is somewhat eroded, which makes it difficult to read. With the assistance of epigrapher Martha Macri, we offer the following partial translation (text 4 p84):

a? yäl? ta? te' [bird?] *yah? ??*
Your throwing down? the Principal Bird Deity? from the tree. Damage to ??.

u ?? [*ajaw w/headband?*] *ta? ?? ??*
It was the ajaw's? ?? in ?? ??.

u? b'ah ma' ch'ahb' ma' ak'ab'
It is the image/face of no genesis, no darkness.

As the translation suggests, the ruler is talking to one (or several) of the figures portrayed on the vessel, who are addressed as "you." He makes reference to a mythological event that is depicted on several well-known pottery vessels, although not on the Miami Vase—that of the Hero Twins defeating a vain and false "sun" in the form of a macaw or falcon, nicknamed by archaeologists the Principal Bird Deity. This was one of the events that set the stage for the peopling of the earth by humans and the creation of a new sun. The text in front of the *ajaw* appears to suggest that this episode can be linked to him in some way.

The final two figures standing behind the ruler are dressed as scribes. The *aj k'uhuun* uniform includes floor-length sarongs, shaved heads with a fringe along the hairline and a long braid down the back, and most important, a scribal headdress that includes writing implements. These significant royal individuals may be witnesses to the ritual being performed nearby and seem to be discussing the progress of the sacred proceedings.

The text on the wall behind the scribes is undeciphered (text 1, p84):

---

rituales y la relación con los demás participantes, el rey alcanza un profundo nivel de conexión con uno de los dioses más importantes del panteón maya. Chahk era responsable de abrir la tierra para que el Dios del Maíz pudiese renacer, lo que representaba un profundo acto de creación del mundo que garantizaba no sólo la continuación de las lluvias anuales para mantener un fructífero ciclo agrícola, sino también la perpetuación de la autoridad real mediante un relato que confería autoridad a los nuevos reyes, que por ende seguían el modelo del Dios del Maíz.

El texto que aparece inmediatamente adelante del gobernante sufrió cierta erosión que dificulta su lectura. Con la ayuda de la epigrafista Martha Macri, ofrecemos la siguiente traducción parcial (texto 4 p84):

¿a? ¿yäl? ¿ta? te' [¿pajaro?] ¿yah? ¿?
¿Has arrojado? ¿la principal deidad pájaro? del árbol. Daños a ¿?.

¿u? [¿ajaw con vincha?] ¿ta? ¿? ¿?
Era el ¿? de ajaw ¿? en ¿? ¿?.

¿u? b'ah ma' ch'ahb' ma' ak'ab'
Es la imagen/el rostro del no génesis, de la no oscuridad.

Como sugiere la traducción, el gobernante está hablando con una (o varias) de las figuras representadas en la vasija, a las que trata en segunda persona (usted/ustedes). Además, hace referencia a un evento mitológico representado en numerosas vasijas de cerámica muy conocidas, aunque no en el Jarrón de Miami: los Héroes Gemelos que vencen a un arrogante y falso "sol" que tiene forma de guacamayo o halcón, al que los arqueólogos apodan "la principal deidad pájaro". Éste era uno de los eventos que habrían sentado las bases para que el hombre poblase la Tierra y para la creación de un nuevo sol. El texto que aparece adelante del *ajaw* parece sugerir que este episodio puede relacionarse con él de algún modo.

Las dos figuras finales que permanecen de pie detrás del gobernante están vestidas como escribas. El uniforme aj *k'uhuun* consta de largas túnicas que llegaban hasta el suelo, cabezas afeitadas con flequillo a lo largo de la línea del pelo, una extensa trenza en la espalda y, lo más importante, un tocado que incluye utensilios de escritura. Estos significativos miembros de la realeza pueden ser testigos del ritual que se lleva a cabo y parecen estar comentando los progresos de los procedimientos sagrados.

si-??-ya nal? ya?-??-ni
?? maize god? ??

The beautiful and complex imagery of the Miami Vase shares a common theme with other codex-style vases known as the "water group" in which the young Maize Deity meets the Hero Twins with ancillary witnesses. The version of this event or ritual depicted on the Miami Vase is much more complex than other examples, and does not take place in a mythological location such as the watery Underworld but in a terrestrial royal palace. Coupled with the obvious human characteristics of the individuals on this vase, it seems likely that this example of the water-group theme shows an assembly of royal men enacting the myth of the rebirth of the Maize Deity through the intersession of the Hero Twins and Chahk. The text of the Miami Vase also departs substantially from what is usually found with water-group vessels, and focuses less on the rank or accomplishments of the individuals depicted and more on the mythological or ritual content of the scene. By stressing the exploits of the Hero Twins and the vanquishing of the false sun of a previous era, the stage is set for the ruler to assume the powers of the deity Chahk within the context of this ritual of resurrection and rebirth. With its beautiful artistry, complicated composition, and lengthy text, the Miami Vase is a unique representation of the sophisticated ceremonial life of royal Maya men, depicting as well the mythology of divinely sanctioned rulers in a culture that believed the maize they ate every day was the body and blood of a precious young god.

For further information:

Coe, Michael D. and Justin Kerr.1998. *The Art of the Maya Scribe.* Harry N. Abrams, New York.

Garcia Barrios, Ana. 2006. "Confrontation Scenes on Codex-Style Pottery: An Iconographic Review." Latin American Indian Literatures Journal 22(2):129-152.

El texto que aparece en la pared detrás de los escribas no pudo descifrarse (text 1, p84):

si- ¿?-ya ¿nal? ¿ya?- ¿?-ni
¿? Dios del Maiz ¿?

Las bellas y complejas imágenes del Jarrón de Miami comparten un tema común con otros vasos de estilo códice que pertenecen al llamado "grupo de agua", en los que la deidad del maíz se encuentra con los Héroes Gemelos y con otros testigos de menor importancia. La versión de este evento o ritual representado en el Jarrón de Miami es mucho más compleja que en otros ejemplos, y no se desarrolla en un lugar mitológico como el inframundo acuático sino en el entorno terrenal de un palacio real. Junto con las evidentes características humanas de las figuras representadas en el jarrón, parece probable que este ejemplo de un tema propio del grupo de agua muestre una escena en la que miembros de la realeza representan el mito del renacer del Dios del Maíz con la intercesión de los Héroes Gemelos y Chahk. El texto del Jarrón de Miami también se diferencia sustancialmente de los elementos que suelen encontrarse en las vasijas del grupo de agua, y no se concentra tanto en la jerarquía ni en los logros de las figuras representadas como en el contenido ritual o mitológico de la escena. Al subrayar las hazañas de los Héroes Gemelos y la derrota del falso sol en una era anterior, se sientan las bases para que el gobernante asuma los poderes de la deidad Chahk en el contexto de este ritual de resurrección y renacimiento. Con su belleza artística, su elaborada composición y sus extensos textos, el Jarrón de Miami constituye una representación única de los sofisticados ceremoniales de los miembros masculinos de la realeza maya, y a la vez describe la mitología de los gobernantes respaldados por los dioses en una cultura en la que se creía que el maíz que se comía cada día era el cuerpo y la sangre de un preciado y joven dios.

Material de consulta para obtener más información:

Coe, Michael D. y Justin Kerr.1998. *The Art of the Maya Scribe.* Harry N. Abrams, New York.

García Barrios, Ana. 2006. "Confrontation Scenes on Codex-Style Pottery: An Iconographic Review." Latin American Indian Literatures Journal 22(2):129-152.

CHAPTER 7:
Divine Beings and Oaxacan Funerary Urns in the Collection of the Lowe Art Museum

Julie K. Wesp

Many of the clay urns from the region of Oaxaca, Mexico, come from funerary contexts, but such urns have also been discovered in dedicatory offerings for temples and other locations not related to burials. The earliest urns appear to have been hand constructed, whereas many of the later examples may have been made by using various molds. Often the urns were left plain, yet some retain the remnants of red, yellow, green, white, and black pigment. Generally, the urns consist of a seated figure with crossed legs, with his or her hands placed on the knees. The hands and feet of the individuals are constructed very simply, while the head and ornamentation have more intricate details. Since many of the cultures of ancient Mesoamerica shared a pantheon of similar deities, various facial features and costume elements are used to identify gods specific to the ceramic urns of Oaxaca.

One of the most commonly represented figures on these urns is the Lightning God, called Cocijo by the Zapotecs (the Aztecs called this deity

CAPITULO 7:
Seres divinos y urnas funerarias de Oaxaca en la colección del Museo de Arte Lowe

Julie K. Wesp

Aunque muchas de las urnas de arcilla de la región de Oaxaca, México, provienen de contextos funerarios, también se han encontrado como ofrendas dedicatorias para templos y otros lugares no relacionados con tumbas. Las urnas más antiguas parecen haber sido hechas a mano, en tanto muchos de los ejemplos posteriores parecen haber sido fabricados mediante el uso de variados moldes. Con frecuencia, las urnas se dejaban sin pintar, aunque algunas conservan restos de pigmentos de color rojo, amarillo, verde, blanco y negro. Por lo general, las urnas consistían en una figura sentada con las piernas cruzadas y las manos apoyadas sobre las rodillas. Las manos y los pies eran de una construcción bastante simple, mientras que la cabeza y los ornamentos tenían detalles más elaborados. Puesto que muchas culturas de la antigua Mesoamérica compartían un panteón común de divinidades, son varias las características faciales y los elementos de vestimenta que se utilizan para identificar a los dioses específicos de las urnas de cerámica de Oaxaca.

Tlaloc, and the Maya, Chahk). This divine being was almost certainly the patron deity of the entire Valley of Oaxaca, evidenced by its strong association with agriculture and its frequent representation at many different sites. The Zapotec people of the Valley relied on maize agriculture to sustain the population. As a result, the deities associated with rain and agriculture were venerated and provided with sacrificial nourishment in order to ensure a plentiful harvest. Other deities associated with agriculture include the Maize Deity (Pitao Cozobi), as discussed elsewhere in this catalog, and the Bat God (Piquite Ziña).

The anthropomorphized image of the Bat God in this exhibition, (2007.52.7, p100), is similar to that on other urns depicting bat deities known from various sites in the Valley of Oaxaca. Called Piquite Ziña by the Zapotecs, the Bat God is one of the mostly widely represented deities, identified on stelae, codices, vases, and whistles. His importance is further evidenced by the fact that his name served as one of the day names in the calendar system. In Mixtec and Aztec codices, priests dressed as bats perform rituals during the month of Ochpaniztli, which is associated with the Maize Deity and fertility. The urn in this exhibition follows common stylistic representations, including a mix of animal and human characteristics. Scholars believe that the majority of bats represented iconographically are from the family *Phyllostomidae* (leaf-nosed bats and vampire bats), found throughout Mesoamerica. The naturalistic representation of a bat head, with the large ears used by bats to echolocate their prey, as well as four incisors and two canine teeth in the upper jaw, helps to identify the individual as the Bat God. The incisors of the lower jaw are covered by the bat's tongue, which is customarily represented projecting from the mouth. The lower portion of the bat's body takes on more human characteristics, including four limbs, with both arms raised and palms facing forward. The figure wears a chest pendant that is typical of human ornamentation and assumes

---

Una de las figuras representadas más habitualmente en estas urnas es el Dios del Rayo, llamado Cocijo por los zapotecas (los aztecas llamaban a esta deidad Tlaloc, y los mayas, Chahk). Es casi seguro que haya sido el dios protector de todo el Valle de Oaxaca, lo que queda evidenciado por su profundo vínculo con la agricultura y sus frecuentes representaciones en muchos sitios diferentes. Los zapotecas del valle requerían del cultivo del maíz para alimentar a la población. Por lo tanto, las deidades asociadas con la lluvia y la agricultura eran veneradas y se les ofrendaban sacrificios para garantizar una cosecha abundante. Otras deidades relacionadas con la agricultura eran el Dios del Maíz (Pitao Cozobi), que se analiza en otras secciones de este catálogo, y el Dios Murciélago (Piquite Ziña).

La imagen antropomorfa del Dios Murciélago que se incluye en esta exhibición (2007.52.7, p100) es similar a la que aparece en otras urnas que representan deidades murciélagos conocidas en diferentes lugares del Valle de Oaxaca. Este dios, llamado Piquite Ziña por los zapotecas, es uno de los más representados y puede observarse en estelas, códices, vasos y silbatos. Su importancia se confirma por el hecho de que su nombre también era uno de los días del sistema calendario. En los códices mixtecas y aztecas, los sacerdotes vestidos como murciélagos realizan rituales durante el mes de Ochpaniztli, el cual se relaciona con el Dios del Maíz y la fertilidad. La urna incluida en esta exhibición muestra representaciones estilísticas comunes, que combinan características animales y humanas. Los expertos creen que la mayoría de los murciélagos representados de forma iconográfica pertenecen a la familia *Phyllostomidae* (murciélagos de nariz con forma de hoja y vampiros), que puede encontrarse en toda Mesoamérica. La representación naturalista de una cabeza de murciélago con las grandes orejas utilizadas para localizar a su presa, y cuatro incisivos y dos caninos en la mandíbula superior, permite identificar a la figura como el Dios Murciélago. Los dientes incisivos de la mandíbula inferior están cubiertos por la lengua del murciélago, que tradicionalmente se representaba saliendo de la boca. La

a masculine identity, wearing a *maxtlatl*, or loincloth.

Some urns depict human figures wearing headdresses that display the characteristics of various deities. One urn in this exhibition, (85.0072, p101), shows a human figure wearing a headdress with stylistic attributes of the Bat God. The individual's posture mimics the distinctive stance of Piquite Ziña, standing with palms facing forward. The emphasis on the bat's palms could be related to the importance of the creature's suction pads, which are used to cling to slippery surfaces. This individual wears a rectangular *maxtlatl*, a chest pendant, and large ear spools. The headdress is a stylistic variation on the Bat God theme, this time represented by the open mouth of the animal. Visible on either side of the mouth are circular images of the bat tragus, the small, pointed, rearward-facing eminence of the external ear. The tragus helps to collect sounds from behind and is critical to the bat's use of echolocation, which enables it to find food. Red and black pigment is preserved on various portions of the surface of this urn. Similar examples of this variant of the Bat God from the site of Monte Alban had traces of red pigment preserved across the face, comparable to a mask.

The third urn in the exhibition, (85.0073, p102), represents the god with the mouth mask of the serpent. Early representations of this deity had a more naturalistic depiction of a serpent's mouth; this urn, however, appears to be from a later period, when artists employed a simpler style. Only the upper jaw of the serpent is represented by a rectangular plate with human-like teeth, and it lacks the distinctive bifurcated tongue of the serpent. The deity wears large ear spools and a cylindrical headdress. The headdress of this deity typically includes Glyph C applied in the center. Scholars have described the two small circles to the left of the glyph as numerals, but the number of circles and their orientation varies on each urn; therefore it is unlikely that the number

---

parte inferior del cuerpo adquiere características más humanas, ya que incluye cuatro extremidades con ambos brazos levantados y las palmas hacia adelante. La figura lleva un pendiente en el torso que es propio de la ornamentación humana y asume una identidad masculina al usar un *maxtlatl* o taparrabos.

Algunas urnas muestran figuras humanas que usan tocados con las características de varias deidades. Una de las urnas de esta exhibición (85.0072, p101) muestra una figura humana que usa un tocado con los atributos estilísticos del Dios Murciélago. La postura imita la posición característica de Piquite Ziña, de pie y con las palmas de las manos hacia adelante. El hincapié en las palmas del murciélago puede relacionarse con la importancia de las almohadillas de succión de esta criatura, que le permiten aferrarse a superficies resbaladizas. Esta figura usa un *maxtlatl* rectangular, un pendiente en el torso y grandes aros en las orejas. El tocado es una variación estilística del tema del Dios Murciélago, esta vez representado por la boca abierta del animal. A ambos lados de la boca pueden verse imágenes circulares del trago del murciélago, la pequeña protuberancia en punta hacia atrás en el oído externo. El trago, le permite al murciélago registrar los sonidos provenientes de atrás y es fundamental para el uso de la ecolocalización para encontrar alimento. En varias partes de la superficie de la urna se conservan pigmentos rojos y negros. Otros ejemplos similares de esta variación del Dios Murciélago provenientes del sitio de Monte Albán muestran rastros de pigmento rojo en el rostro, en lo que puede compararse con una máscara.

La tercera urna de la exhibición (85.0073, p102) representa al dios con una máscara con la forma de la boca de una serpiente. Las primeras representaciones de esta deidad mostraban un estilo más naturalista de la boca de la serpiente. Sin embargo, esta urna parece ser de un período posterior, en el que los artistas empleaban un estilo más simple. Sólo la mandíbula superior de la serpiente está representada por una placa rectangular con dientes que parecen humanos, sin la

indicates the name of the deity. On either side of this glyph is the representation of a corncob, another characteristic that is only found on urns from later periods. Protruding from either side of the face are representations of a serpent in profile. The figure wears a chest pendant in the form of a circle with four rectangles extending beyond his shoulders and knees, a stylized flower projecting downward over the loincloth, and a cape draped across his shoulders.

These vessels from the Lowe's permanent collection are excellent examples, each displaying key features of Oaxacan funerary urns. Iconographic analysis of the intricate details on these urns provides insight into the various deities that were important in ancient Zapotec culture and their relationship to the natural forces that surrounded daily life for the ancient population of the Valley of Oaxaca.

For further information:

Caso, Alfonso and Ignacio Bernal. 1952. *Urnas de Oaxaca*. Instituto Nacional de Antropología e Historia, Mexico.

Whitecotton, Joseph W. 1977. *The Zapotecs: Princes, Priests, and Peasants*. University of Oklahoma Press, Norman.

---

característica lengua bifurcada. La deidad lleva grandes aros en las orejas y un tocado cilíndrico. Habitualmente, el tocado de esta deidad incluye el glifo C aplicado en el centro. Si bien los académicos han descrito los dos pequeños círculos que aparecen a la izquierda del glifo como signos numéricos, la cantidad de círculos y su orientación varían en cada urna. Por lo tanto, es poco probable que el número indique el nombre de la deidad. A ambos lados del glifo aparece la representación de una mazorca, otra característica que sólo se encuentra en urnas de períodos tardíos. Las protuberancias a ambos lados del rostro representan el perfil de una serpiente. La figura lleva un pendiente en el torso con forma de círculo y con cuatro rectángulos que se extienden más allá de los hombros y las rodillas, una flor estilizada que se proyecta por encima del taparrabos y una capa que cuelga de los hombros.

Estas vasijas pertenecientes a la colección permanente del Museo Lowe son excelentes ejemplos de las principales características de las urnas funerarias de Oaxaca. El análisis iconográfico de los intrincados detalles de estas urnas ofrece valiosa información sobre las diferentes deidades que eran importantes para la cultura zapoteca y su relación con las fuerzas de la naturaleza que influían en la vida diaria de los antiguos habitantes del Valle de Oaxaca.

Material de consulta para obtener más información:

Caso, Alfonso e Ignacio Bernal. 1952. *Urnas de Oaxaca*. Instituto Nacional de Antropología e Historia, México.

Whitecotton, Joseph W. 1977. *The Zapotecs: Princes, Priests, and Peasants*. University of Oklahoma Press, Norman.

CHAPTER 8:
Marine Life in the Art of Ancient Parita Bay, Panama

Erica Sefton

Pre-Columbian America, from central Mexico through South America, is best understood as a continuum of shared goods and culture. Within this wide continuum there existed two major cultural spheres: Mesoamerica and the Andean lands. These cultures had minimal direct contact, though certain cultural similarities existed between the two. Situated in the middle of these spheres is a region known as the Intermediate Area, what is now Costa Rica, Panama, and Colombia. The best-known cultures from the area remained independent of the major empires to their north and south, although it is believed they provided a cultural link in certain ways. The more complex social organization seen in the empires allowed for greater social stratification and an increased importance on elite status items. In comparison, the Intermediate Area groups were organized in less-stratified societies known as chiefdoms.

Here, a greater degree of artistic expression is seen on common and utilitarian objects,

---

CAPITULO 8:
Vida marina en el arte antiguo de la bahía de Parita, Panamá

Erica Sefton

La América precolombina, desde la parte central de México hasta América del Sur, se entiende mejor como un continuo de bienes y culturas compartidas. En este escenario ininterrumpido existieron dos grandes esferas culturales: Mesoamérica y la zona Andina. Estas culturas tuvieron un mínimo contacto directo, aunque compartieron algunas similitudes. Entre estas dos culturas existe una zona conocida como el Área Intermedia, que abarca los actuales territorios de Costa Rica, Panamá y Colombia. Las culturas más conocidas de esta zona se desarrollaron en forma independiente de los grandes imperios del norte y del sur, aunque se cree que en ciertos aspectos actuaron como un enlace cultural. Las organizaciones de mayor complejidad social de los grandes imperios daban lugar a una estratificación social más profunda, lo que aumentaba la importancia de los objetos que señalaban el estatus de la élite. En comparación, los grupos que habitaron el Área Intermedia se organizaron en sociedades menos estratificadas conocidas como cacicazgos.

compared with the art of the empires, because fewer full-time specialists were supported and a greater percentage of the population had time to create art for their own purposes. The heart of the Intermediate Area is modern-day Panama. Modern international boundaries do not reflect the pre-Columbian cultural territories, and the major cultural groups of Panama extended north into southern Costa Rica, the Diquis Zone, and south into northern Colombia. This area is best known throughout the region for its exquisite gold work. Much of the trade between the empires and these smaller groups was for status items such as gold and copper metalwork. Pottery, however, was also prized as both an artistic and utilitarian item that would commonly be traded within and outside the region. Panamanian pottery is most similar to the styles of northern Costa Rica and South America, though it is unique in its common use of asymmetrical forms and its tendency toward favoring the colors gray and purple, likely a reflection of the natural environment.

Sites along the coast of Parita Bay, located on the northwest corner of the Gulf of Panama, provide exceptional examples of art reflecting both shared cultural influences and inspiration from the natural world. The coast is shallow and silt-filled, and the environment is mostly composed of mangroves, swamps, marshes, and salt flats. The people here typically subsisted on mollusks, crustaceans, and fish. As a result, these marine motifs dominate artistic expression. Two ceramic pieces from this area represented in the exhibition, (89.0081, p152 and 89.0082, p153), are similar to each other, yet remain distinct from the other Panamanian and Intermediate Area objects on display. They bear some resemblance to the bowls and vases of Mesoamerica, though the motifs represented are specific to the Parita Bay environment. The first piece, 89.0081, is a dish with a she-crab motif, portrayed in colors that mirror the environment. The gray color is likely a reflection of the salt flats and swampy locale, while the purple and reddish colors reflect the animals most often seen in the region

---

Si se compara con el arte de los grandes imperios, en esta zona se observa un mayor grado de expresiones artísticas en objetos utilitarios de uso común debido a que no había tantos especialistas de tiempo completo y un gran porcentaje de la población tenía tiempo para crear piezas de arte para fines propios. El núcleo del Área Intermedia es la zona donde actualmente se encuentra Panamá. Las actuales fronteras internacionales no reflejan los territorios culturales precolombinos, y los principales grupos culturales de Panamá se extendían hacia el norte hasta llegar al sur de Costa Rica (la zona de Diquís) y hacia el sur hasta alcanzar el norte de Colombia. Esta zona es muy conocida por sus exquisitas piezas de oro. Gran parte del comercio entre los grandes imperios y estos pequeños grupos estaba dedicado a los objetos de estatus, como las artesanías en oro y cobre. No obstante, las piezas de alfarería también eran valoradas como objetos artísticos y utilitarios, y habitualmente se comercializaban dentro y fuera de la región. Las cerámicas panameñas tienen un estilo muy similar al de las piezas del norte de Costa Rica y América del Sur, aunque son únicas por el amplio uso de formas asimétricas y la tendencia a privilegiar los colores gris y púrpura, probablemente como un reflejo del entorno natural.

Los sitios ubicados a lo largo de la costa de la bahía de Parita, en el extremo noroeste del Golfo de Panamá, ofrecen extraordinarios ejemplos de piezas de arte que reflejan tanto las influencias culturales compartidas como la inspiración en el mundo de la naturaleza. La costa, poco profunda y con sedimentos arcillosos, está compuesta principalmente por manglares, pantanos, ciénagas y salinas. Sus habitantes se alimentaban de moluscos, crustáceos y peces. Como consecuencia de esto, los motivos marinos dominaron las expresiones artísticas. Dos piezas de cerámica de esta zona que forman parte de la exhibición (89.0081, p152 y 89.0082, p153) comparten grandes similitudes entre sí y a la vez se diferencian del resto de los objetos de Panamá y el Área Intermedia que se exponen. Tienen cierto parecido con los tazones y vasos de Mesoamérica, aunque los motivos representados son

such as crabs and other marine life. The cream-colored slip was applied to the whole surface of the dish, followed by the design colors. Once fired, the design was polished to deepen the color on the final product. Also typical of Parita Bay polychromes, the corners and line endings are finely tipped points showing purposeful care in the design element.

The second piece, 89.0082, is a pedestal dish with a catfish motif. Again, marine life provides the most immediate inspiration for groups in this area. These people were more threatened by marine predators such as sharks, rays, and large predatory fish, compared with inland groups that were threatened by land predators such as jaguars and large reptiles. The concentric bands around the edge of the dish are typical of a widespread stylistic feature of ceramics in this region. Ceramic pieces on pedestals are quite common in this region, especially from sites around Parita Bay, though globular-shaped tops are much more frequently seen; the flat, dish-shaped top on this piece is quite unusual. The materials, shape, and form of these pottery pieces reflect cultural influences, especially from the north and the cultures of the Diquis Zone. Costa Rican pottery was highly valued and extensively traded even in pre-Columbian times. By aspiring to produce pottery of a comparable high quality, these people had more trading power with the surrounding groups, which in turn increased the cultural diffusion throughout the area.

The marrying of natural and human environments provides the inspiration for great art, and in Parita Bay this blend takes on a singular and beautiful form. The abstract depictions of marine life on high-quality, though basic, pottery forms, is particular to Parita Bay, but still representative of the Intermediate Area—a region that was well known in both the northern and southern cultural spheres, though not fully a part of either.

---

específicos del entorno de la bahía de Parita. La pieza 89.0081 es un plato con el motivo de un cangrejo hembra, pintado en colores que reflejan los colores del entorno natural. El color gris imita las salinas y los pantanos locales, en tanto el púrpura y los tonos rojizos reflejan los colores de los animales más vistos en la región, como el cangrejo y otros habitantes de la vida marina. Un suave tono crema se aplicó en toda la superficie del plato, sobre la que se pintaron los colores del diseño. Una vez horneado, el diseño se pulió para profundizar los colores en el producto final. Las esquinas y los bordes, también típicos de las piezas policromáticas de la bahía de Parita, están delicadamente marcados con puntos, lo que muestra un cuidado deliberado por el elemento del diseño.

La segunda pieza (89.0082) es un plato pedestal con el motivo de un bagre. Nuevamente, la vida marina ofrece una fuente de inspiración inmediata para los grupos de esta zona. Estos pueblos estaban más amenazados por los depredadores marinos como los tiburones, rayas y grandes peces, en comparación con los grupos de tierra adentro cuya amenaza principal eran los depredadores terrestres como los jaguares y grandes reptiles. Las bandas concéntricas que se observan en los bordes del plato son características de un estilo de cerámica muy extendido en la región. Las piezas de cerámica sobre pedestales son muy comunes en esta región, especialmente en sitios cercanos a la bahía de Parita, aunque la parte superior de las piezas tiene con mayor frecuencia una forma globular, y es por eso que la parte superior plana y con forma de plato de esta pieza es muy poco usual. Los materiales y las formas de estas piezas de cerámica reflejan diversas influencias culturales, especialmente del norte y de las culturas de la zona de Diquís. La alfarería de Costa Rica era muy apreciada y comercializada en los tiempos precolombinos. Al aspirar a crear piezas comparables por su alta calidad, estos pueblos aumentaron su comercio con los grupos circundantes, lo que a su vez aumentó la difusión cultural en toda la región.

El profundo vínculo del entorno humano y

For further information:

Linares, Olga F. 1977. *Ecology and the Arts in Ancient Panama: On the Development of Social Rank and Symbolism in the Central Provinces.* Dumbarton Oaks, Washington, DC.

Stone, Rebecca. 2002. *Seeing With New Eyes: Highlights of the Michael C. Carlos Museum Collection of Art of the Ancient Americas.* Michael C. Carlos Museum, Emory University, Atlanta.

---

natural ofrece una fuente de inspiración para grandes obras de arte, y en la bahía de Parita esta combinación toma una bella y singular forma. Las representaciones abstractas de la vida marina en piezas de cerámica básicas pero de alta calidad son características de la bahía de Parita, y también un ejemplo del arte del Área Intermedia, una región muy renombrada en las esferas culturales del norte y del sur, aunque sin pertenecer completamente a ninguna.

Material de consulta para obtener más información:

Linares, Olga F. 1977. *Ecology and the Arts in Ancient Panama: On the Development of Social Rank and Symbolism in the Central Provinces.* Dumbarton Oaks, Washington, DC.

Stone, Rebecca. 2002. *Seeing With New Eyes: Highlights of the Michael C. Carlos Museum Collection of Art of the Ancient Americas.* Michael C. Carlos Museum, Emory University, Atlanta.

CHAPTER 9:
Chicomecoatl, the Aztec Maize Goddess

Gretel Rodríguez

The peoples of ancient Mesoamerica maintained a vital and reciprocal relationship with their natural environment. The many plants and animals that ensured their survival were symbolized by an array of gods and goddesses that constituted the center of complex ceremonial practices. Maize, as the most important staple food in the Americas, was revered in the form of numerous deities, who symbolically conveyed the different aspects of the plant's natural growing stages. Among the most recurring representations of maize are the sculptures of Chicomecoatl, a goddess found primarily in the Central Valley of Mexico, who symbolized the ripe maize plant and, more generally, the concept of sustenance for the ancient Aztecs. A beautiful example of this ubiquitous Mesoamerican sculptural type on display in this exhibition (56.003.000, p110), is from the permanent collection of the Lowe Art Museum. While representative of the essential characteristics of Aztec sculpture, the piece also provides useful information about the ideology and daily lives

---

CAPITULO 9:
Chicomecóatl, la diosa azteca del maíz

Gretel Rodríguez

Los pueblos de la Mesoamérica antigua mantenían un vínculo vital y recíproco con su entorno natural. Las numerosas plantas y animales que les brindaban sustento eran simbolizados por una serie de dioses y diosas que constituían el centro de complejas prácticas ceremoniales. El maíz, el principal alimento básico de América, era reverenciado a través de numerosas deidades que simbólicamente comunicaban los diversos aspectos de las etapas de crecimiento de esta planta. Entre las representaciones más reiteradas del maíz se encuentran las esculturas de Chicomecóatl, una diosa que principalmente se adoraba en la región del Valle Central de México y que simbolizaba la planta de maíz madura y, de forma más general, el concepto del sustento entre los antiguos aztecas. Un bello ejemplo de este ubicuo tipo de escultura mesoamericana presente en esta exhibición (56.003.000, p110), pertenece a la colección permanente del Museo de Arte Lowe. Si bien es representativa de las características esenciales de la escultura azteca, la pieza también proporciona información de

of the peoples of ancient Mesoamerica.

The art of the Aztecs, like most of the artistic production of ancient Mesoamerica, had a predominantly religious character. Art served as an important vehicle to communicate religious principles through visual means, and training in the arts was regarded as prestigious by members of the ruling elites. This direct connection between art and ritual can be seen in the great monumental sculptures that have been found associated with temples and large ceremonial centers at the Aztec capital of Tenochtitlan. Another trend of smaller-scale sculpture, however, with clear regional and domestic connotations, coexisted with the more imperial-oriented convention. Because of its modest dimensions and simple carving style, the image of Chicomecoatl at the Lowe, can be placed in the latter category.

Although jade and obsidian were used in small-scale luxury objects, larger-scale sculpture was made predominately of basalt, and most pieces were originally covered in plaster and painted. The most significant features of Aztec sculpture are the fine carving technique, an emphasis on roundness and three-dimensionality, an interest in naturalistic representations, and the depiction of figures in static, symmetric positions. Human figures, animals, and gods are the most recurring themes. Calendric glyphs and other forms of script were frequently carved in bas-relief as part of their decoration. Despite the great realism achieved by Aztec stone artists, the main function of Aztec sculpture was symbolic, and most images were integrated into ritual practices.

The earliest accounts of the cult of Chicomecoatl come from the Spanish Franciscan friar and pre-modern amateur ethnographer, Bernardino de Sahagún. In his copious chronicles of life in the Aztec empire, Sahagún describes in detail the rituals associated with the maize harvest, noting that the celebration was "in honor of the goddess called Chicomecoatl, whom they imagined as a woman and they said she was the one who

---

gran utilidad sobre la ideología y la vida diaria en la Mesoamérica antigua.

El arte de los aztecas, al igual que la mayoría de la producción artística de Mesoamérica, tenía un carácter predominantemente religioso. El arte servía como un importante vehículo para comunicar los principios religiosos por medios visuales, y la educación artística se consideraba un símbolo de prestigio entre los miembros de las élites gobernantes. La relación directa entre arte y ritual puede verse claramente en las grandiosas y monumentales esculturas que fueron halladas en los templos y grandes centros ceremoniales de la capital azteca de Tenochtitlán. Sin embargo, junto con estas prácticas de orientación imperial, también existió otra tendencia de esculturas de menor escala con claras connotaciones regionales y domésticas. Debido a sus modestas dimensiones y su estilo simple, la imagen de Chicomecóatl que se exhibe en el Lowe puede incluirse en esta segunda categoría.

Si bien el jade y la obsidiana se utilizaban en objetos de lujo de pequeña escala, las esculturas de mayor envergadura se realizaban casi siempre en basalto, y la mayoría de las piezas originalmente estaban cubiertas con yeso y pintadas. Las características más significativas de la escultura azteca son la delicada técnica de cincelado, el hincapié en las formas redondeadas y la tridimensionalidad, el interés por las representaciones naturalistas y el uso de figuras en posiciones estáticas y simétricas. Las figuras humanas, los animales y los dioses eran los temas más recurrentes. Los glifos relacionados con el calendario y otras formas de escritura con frecuencia se tallaban en bajorrelieve como parte de la decoración. A pesar del gran realismo alcanzado por los escultores aztecas, la principal función de las esculturas era simbólica y la mayoría de las imágenes se incorporaban a prácticas rituales.

Los primeros testimonios del culto a Chicomecóatl provienen del sacerdote franciscano español Bernardino de Sahagún, pionero de la etnografía moderna. En sus numerosas crónicas sobre la vida en el Imperio Azteca, Sahagún

gave the sustenance for the body, in order to preserve human life…" Despite some ambiguity in his description of the deity's visual forms, several basic elements are consistent in his account and in the material record, such as the red pigment used on her body and face, the paper headdress that she invariably wears, and the ears of maize she usually holds in her hands.

The imagery associated with Chicomecoatl is highly standardized, making the deity easily recognizable. Within this standardization, however, Aztec artists also left room for the expression of their extensive imaginative range. The most distinctive iconographic element that identifies the images of Chicomecoatl is the quadrangular "temple" headdress, called *amacalli*, which was made of paper bands and adorned with pleated paper rosettes. Other items commonly associated with this deity are the typical skirt or *huipilli* with embroidered or painted flowers, the *quechquemitl* or female's triangular blouse, and a greenstone necklace. In most cases, the goddess holds two maize ears in each hand, but in some examples she holds a shaft or a ritual rattle, which was associated with fertility.

The image of Chicomecoatl at the Lowe is a fine example of Aztec freestanding sculpture. Carved in basalt, like most of the surviving pieces, this sculpture shows the standardized features that are common to most Chicomecoatl representations. The female figure, which represents the goddess, or perhaps a human impersonator, stands immobile with her arms extended to the front. The small body is practically subsumed by the imposing rectangular *amacalli*; the figure's face emerges from this headdress, which occupies nearly half of the total volume of the piece. Minute traces of pigment on the stone's surface suggest the use of red-colored paint typical of these works. The headdress is adorned with two large rosettes, and two segments of rope tied in a large knot hold the piece together.

Compared to other Chicomecoatl representa-

---

describe en detalle los rituales vinculados con la cosecha del maíz y destaca que la celebración se realizaba "en honor de la diosa llamada Chicomecóatl, la cual imaginaban como mujer y decían, era ella la que daba los mantenimientos del cuerpo, para conservar la vida humana…". A pesar de cierta ambigüedad en su descripción de las formas visuales de la deidad, varios elementos básicos de sus relatos coinciden con los registros materiales, como el pigmento rojo utilizado en el cuerpo y el rostro de la diosa, el tocado de papel que siempre usa y las mazorcas de maíz que generalmente sostiene en sus manos.

El imaginario asociado a Chicomecóatl es muy estandarizado, por lo que es muy fácil reconocer a esta diosa. Sin embargo, en el marco de esta estandarización, los artistas aztecas también tenían lugar para expresar su amplio espectro imaginativo. El elemento iconográfico más característico que permite identificar las imágenes de Chicomecóatl es el tocado cuadrangular o "tocado de templo" denominado *amacalli*, que estaba hecho de tiras de papel y adornado con rosetas de papel plegado. Otros elementos habitualmente relacionados con esta deidad son la falda típica o *huipilli* con flores bordadas o pintadas, el *quechquemitl*, que es una blusa de forma triangular, y un collar de cuentas de color verde. En la mayoría de los casos, la diosa sostiene dos mazorcas de maíz en cada mano, aunque en algunos ejemplos porta una lanza o un sonajero ritual que estaba vinculado con la fertilidad.

La imagen de Chicomecóatl que se exhibe en el Lowe es un gran ejemplo de la escultura tridimensional azteca. Tallada en basalto como la mayoría de las piezas que se han encontrado, la escultura muestra las características estandarizadas que son comunes a la mayoría de las representaciones de Chicomecóatl. La figura femenina que representa a la diosa, o quizás a un humano que la personifica, permanece de pie, estática, con los brazos extendidos hacia adelante. El pequeño cuerpo está prácticamente cubierto por el imponente tocado rectangular o *amacalli*; el rostro de la figura emerge del to-

tions, the one at the Lowe is remarkable for its simplicity in both manufacture and decoration. The carving work is delicate but spare, and the ornamentation is considerably more austere than in other representational images. Facial features are barely delineated, with slit eyes and prominent nose and lips. The idea of clothing is only suggested by a rope that gracefully ties her *huipilli* above the waist. Contrary to other representations of the deity, she lacks obvious breasts, which are commonly related to fertility. Her hands and feet are carved in detail, but both seem disproportionately large for her body.

This interest in highlighting the hands is not an isolated occurrence in Aztec sculpture. The frontal and rigid position of arms and hands is similar to that of the renowned "standard-bearer" figures, which have been found frequently among Central Mexican sculpture, and can be seen in the sculpture of the god Xipe Totec (2008.39.20, p117) in the exhibition. An equally recurrent trait, but more specific to the images of Chicomecoatl, are the two pairs of maize ears that she holds in each hand. These corn ears symbolize the ones that, according to Sahagún, were ritually offered to the goddess by a group of virgins during the yearly harvest ritual. The representation of this trait shows some variation, with some pieces depicting well-defined ears with visible grains, while others show them in a more stylized or conceptual manner. The latter is the case in the Chicomecoatl at the Lowe, in which the maize ears are smooth and plain, also suggesting two pairs of ritual rattles. In light of the highly symbolic character of Aztec sculpture, it seems logical to assume that the objects held by this Chicomecoatl figure are in fact highly stylized representations of the maize plant. The extended arms holding the maize ears also serve as a structural element, which adds support to the large headdress piece.

A tentative exploration of this sculpture's main function is possible through an analysis of its essential visual forms. Although other ex-

---

cado que ocupa casi la mitad del volumen total de la pieza. Pequeños trazos de pigmento en la superficie de piedra sugieren el uso de pintura de color rojo, habitual en estas obras. El tocado está adornado con dos grandes rosetas, y dos trozos de cuerda atados con un gran nudo mantienen unida la pieza.

En comparación con otras representaciones de Chicomecóatl, la que se exhibe en el Lowe es notable por su simplicidad de fabricación y decoración. El tallado es delicado pero mínimo, y la ornamentación es considerablemente más austera que en otras imágenes figurativas. Los rasgos faciales están apenas delineados, con dos breves cortes por ojos y labios y nariz prominentes. El ropaje apenas está sugerido por una cuerda que con gracia sujeta su *huipilli* alrededor de la cintura. A diferencia de otras representaciones de la deidad, no muestra senos voluminosos, que suelen relacionarse con el concepto de fertilidad. Sus manos y sus pies están tallados en detalle, aunque parecen desproporcionadamente grandes para el cuerpo.

Este interés en destacar las manos no es un caso aislado en la escultura azteca. La posición frontal y rígida de las manos es similar a la de las renombradas figuras de "porta estandartes" encontradas con frecuencia en la escultura de la región central de México y también puede verse en la escultura del dios Xipe Totec (2008.39.20, p117) incluida en la exhibición. Otro rasgo que también se repite, pero más específicamente en las imágenes de Chicomecóatl, son los dos pares de mazorcas de maíz que sostiene en cada mano. Las mazorcas simbolizan a las que, según el testimonio de Sahagún, eran ofrecidas como ritual a la diosa por un grupo de vírgenes durante la ceremonia anual de la cosecha. La representación de este rasgo muestra variaciones, y algunas piezas representan mazorcas bien delineadas y con granos visibles, en tanto otras las muestran de forma más estilizada o conceptual. Este último es el caso de la representación de Chicomecóatl exhibida en el Lowe, en la que las mazorcas de maíz son simples y llanas, sugiriendo también dos pares de sonajeros rituales. A la luz de la naturaleza altamente simbólica

amples of Chicomecoatl are considerably more sophisticated in ornamentation and detail, the Lowe's piece, while maintaining the goddess's main attributes and shape, is remarkable for its minimalism. This overall simplicity in style and dimensions suggests that it was intended for a local or domestic shrine. The distinctive standardization of Chicomecoatl's iconography has been correlated to mass production and its wide distribution throughout Central Mexico. Conforming to this concept, the small scale and simple manufacture of this Chicomecoatl indicate that it was probably intended to be an object of mass consumption. Moreover, due to its symbolic associations with fertility, this small sculpture could have been used at a domestic altar in order to ensure the family's daily sustenance as well as numerous and healthy progeny.

Though traditionally considered a minor goddess, Chicomecoatl's importance derives from her essential role in the daily lives of Aztec people. Whereas other deities with imperial associations such as Huitzilopochtli or Tláloc were more visible at state-level rituals, a goddess like Chicomecoatl is clearly associated with a domestic ceremonial context. Her cult was described in detail by Bernardino de Sahagún, whose early ethnohistorical account revealed the significance of her festival for the peoples of pre-Columbian Mexico. The goddess's strong connection with maize, a plant regarded by all peoples of the Americas as essential for their survival, transcends private ritual function and further associates the deity with the wider concept of earth's fertility. At the same time, small Chicomecoatl representations such as this fine example, serve as a reminder of the importance of agricultural deities in the ritual life of complex societies, and opens up a more individualized look at the life of common people who populated the great cities and the smaller towns of ancient Mesoamerica.

---

de la escultura azteca, parece lógico suponer que los objetos sostenidos por esta figura de Chicomecóatl en realidad son representaciones muy estilizadas de la planta del maíz. Los brazos extendidos que sostienen las mazorcas también sirven como elemento estructural, lo que agrega apoyo para la enorme pieza del tocado.

Por medio del análisis de las formas visuales básicas de esta escultura es posible arriesgar una explicación tentativa sobre su función principal. Si bien otros ejemplos de representación de Chicomecóatl son mucho más sofisticados en ornamentación y detalles, la pieza exhibida en el Lowe no sólo mantiene los principales atributos y formas de la diosa sino que es notable por su minimalismo. Esta simplicidad general de estilo y dimensiones sugiere que la escultura estaba diseñada para utilizarse en un lugar sagrado local o doméstico. La característica estandarización de la iconografía de Chicomecóatl ha sido correlacionada con la producción en masa y su amplia distribución en toda la región del centro de México. De acuerdo con este concepto, la fabricación simple y en pequeña escala de esta escultura de Chicomecóatl indica que probablemente estaba dirigida a ser un objeto de consumo masivo. Aun más, debido a sus asociaciones simbólicas con la fertilidad, existe la posibilidad de que esta pequeña escultura se haya utilizado en un altar doméstico para asegurar el sustento diario de la familia al igual que una numerosa y saludable descendencia.

Si bien tradicionalmente se la considera una diosa de menor jerarquía, la importancia de Chicomecóatl radica en su papel esencial en la vida diaria del pueblo azteca. Mientras que otras deidades con connotaciones imperiales como Huitzilopochtli o Tláloc eran más visibles en los rituales del estado, una diosa como Chicomecóatl se relaciona claramente con el contexto ceremonial doméstico. Su culto es descrito detalladamente por Bernardino de Sahagún, cuyos tempranos registros etnohistóricos revelan la trascendencia de su festival para los pueblos de México en la etapa precolombina. La fuerte conexión de esta diosa con la planta del maíz,

For more information:

Pasztory, Esther. 1983. *Aztec Art*. Harry N. Abrams, Inc. Publishers, New York.

Solís, Felipe. 2003. "El Hombre Frente a la Naturaleza Mítica" in: *Dioses del México Antiguo*, E. Matos Moctezuma, editor: 91-99. Editorial Océano, México.

---

considerada por todos los pueblos americanos como un alimento esencial para la supervivencia, trasciende el ritual privado para vincular a esta deidad con un concepto más amplio de fertilidad de la tierra. Al mismo tiempo, las pequeñas representaciones de Chicomecóatl como la de este bello ejemplo sirven para recordarnos la importancia de las deidades agrícolas en la vida ritual de las sociedades complejas y brindan una visión más individualizada sobre la vida del hombre común que habitaba las grandes ciudades y los pequeños pueblos de la antigua Mesoamérica.

Material de consulta para obtener más información:

Pasztory, Esther. 1983. *Aztec Art*. Harry N. Abrams, Inc. Publishers, New York.

Solís, Felipe. 2003. "El Hombre Frente a la Naturaleza Mítica" en: *Dioses del México Antiguo*, E. Matos Moctezuma, editor: 91-99. Editorial Océano, México.

OLMEC

OLMEC
Formative Period, 1200-600 BCE

The Olmec heartland is centered in the wetlands of Veracruz and Tabasco along the southern Gulf of Mexico. This fertile area provided a rich environment for nascent agriculturalists, and Olmec civilization is known as the Mother Culture for its profound influence upon all later cultures of ancient Mesoamerica. Corn agriculture, funerary pyramids, animal-human supernaturals, and especially the use of translucent jade to symbolize life force all originated with the Olmec and continued for millennia. The swampy conditions of the Olmec heartland make their centers difficult to visit but much of their powerful art is preserved in museum collections.

The colossal stone heads that are a well known component of Olmec art represent rulers and are some of the earliest noble portraits in Mesoamerica. Fashioned from basalt boulders, these heads often weigh many tons and may depict these leaders as ballplayers. Other figural art depicts a wide variety of supernatural creatures and the pan-Mesoamerican tradition of animal companions or spirit helpers can be seen in the were-jaguars, caimans, harpy eagles, and serpents that appear so often in Olmec sculpture. Leadership may have had a strong shamanic component, with clan elders who drew upon the power of their animal totem. Olmec figurines included in this exhibition show the loose body stance of shamans in trance, and hallucinogens are known to have been consumed by religious specialists.

One of the great mysteries of the Olmec is how they perfected stone carving so early in their history. All stone had to be imported into the region, and the source for the blue jade the Olmec preferred is far away in the highlands of Guatemala. Using only quartz sand and other stone, artists created finely nuanced stone sculptures in some of the hardest minerals known, without the use of metal tools. Despite a concentration along the Gulf Coast, Olmec art and influence spread throughout Mesoamerica as far as the highlands of Mexico and Costa Rica.

Celt
Olmec (Gulf Coast, Mexico)
ca. 1500-400 BCE
Jade
6 １/₂ x 2 ⁷/₈ x ⁷/₈"
Gift of Mr. and Mrs. Barry Fitzmorris, 2005.29.6

The use of jade to create luxurious portable objects in a great variety in styles and dimensions began in the Olmec period. This piece is an excellent example of the fine lapidary technique achieved by early artisans and displays the principal iconographic elements of the Olmec style. The figure is carved in the shape of an axe head, although it clearly was not intended for a utilitarian purpose. Almond shaped eyes are surmounted by arched eyebrows which slope down following the line of a cleft in the forehead. The nose is wide and the snarling mouth, perhaps the most distinctive trait, opens with a curled upper lip to show a pair of "fangs" at each corner. The contours of arms and legs have been incised into the figure, helping achieve a harmonious balance of two and three-dimensional elements in the piece. Folded arms cover the chest, as if holding an object. Several perforations in the corners of the mouth, the hands, and the ears, probably were inlaid with shell or some other contrasting material. A variety of interpretations have been suggested for this type of Olmec jade figure. It has long been proposed that they represent the combined features of a human baby and a feline, a sort of mythological "were-jaguar," with the cleft forehead representing vegetation emerging from the earth, or simply certain anatomical traits of jaguars. Other interpretations link the cleft with the regenerative process by which a toad sheds its skin, a natural occurrence interpreted by ancient Mesoamerican people as a reenactment of earth's ecological cycles. The large repertoire of hybridized supernatural beings in Olmec art demonstrates a complex understanding of how power could be visually represented in metaphors drawn from the surrounding natural environment. This beautiful jade piece conveys authority both through the precious material of jade, but also through reference to the powers of the natural world.

Sources: Furst (1981), Miller (2006)

Dragon
Olmec (Gulf Coast, Mexico)
ca. 1500–400 BCE
Basalt stone
12 5/8 x 13 5/8 x 18 1/2"
Gift of Edward R. Roberts, 2006.31.1

The dragon is the most significant zoomorphic creature represented in Olmec art. This being, a hybrid of a caiman and a harpy eagle, symbolically conveys the idea of movement through earth, water, and sky. Some of the visual traits most commonly associated with this iconic creature are the "L" shaped eyes, the flame eyebrows, the "hand-paw" motif to indicate the limbs, and the toothless gums. The basalt sculpture of an Olmec dragon in the collection of the Lowe has a reptilian or amphibian body and eyes surmounted by "flame eyebrows." The nose is suggested by a pair of half-circles and a bifid tongue emerges from the toothless mouth. The four limbs are barely cut into the rock. As in most such representations the animal is portrayed in a resting, crouching position, with the head up and the extremities attached to the body. Some unusual traits make this piece unique, such as the overall rounded shape and the depiction of the lower jaw. Though usually represented with the body of a crocodile or iguana, this Olmec dragon incorporates the image of a toad, an animal that in Olmec art has associations with earth, longevity, and fertility.

Sources: Miller (2006), *PAUM* (1995)

Necklace
Olmec (Gulf Coast, Mexico)
ca. 1500–400 BCE
Jadeite, rock crystal, shell and pyrite
12 1/8"
Gift of Edward R. Roberts, 2006.31.13

Jewelry was used as an important indication of status by Mesoamerican peoples from very early times. This necklace is constructed using beads and pendants of several luxury materials such as rock crystal, spondylus shell, pyrite and jadeite. Luxury artifacts of Olmec style and manufacture such as jade celts and necklaces have been found throughout Mesoamerica in regions as distant as Honduras and central Mexico. This is an important indication of the great prestige attached to Olmec ideology and crafts, a culture that helped shape the traditions of many later societies, including the Maya and the Aztecs.

Sources: Miller (2006)

Figure
Olmec (Gulf Coast, Mexico)
ca. 1500-400 BCE
Jade
2 3/4 x 1 x 1 5/8"
Gift of The Rubin - Ladd Foundation, 2007.4.13

This miniature figure is skillfully carved in jade, the most prized stone in ancient Mesoamerica. It represents a highly abstracted hybrid of human and zoomorphic attributes. The lower part suggests the legs and torso of a male human figure. Though highly simplified, the proportions accurately imitate correct anatomical form. The upper part depicts a zoomorphic head, with a long snout and a drilled hole at the center. Two elongated arms hold the upper part of the sculpture, suggesting a mask or headgear. The combination of human and animal forms in order to represent supernatural beings was an important convention within Olmec art, and the representation of humans wearing animal masks was used throughout Mesoamerica as a symbol of animistic ritual practices. This image might represent a shaman wearing the mask of his animal avatar.

Sources: *PAUM* (1995)

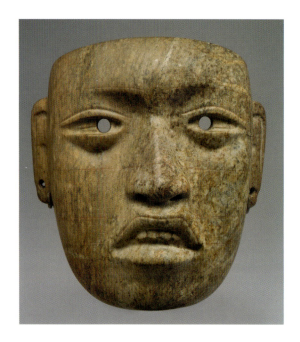

Mask
Olmec (Gulf Coast, Mexico)
ca. 1500-400 BCE
Greenstone
7 5/8 x 7 3/8 x 4 3/8"
Gift of Mr. and Mrs. Barry Fitzmorris, 2009.5

Perhaps a portrait or death mask of an historic individual, this greenstone mask displays a great sensitivity to the natural features of a human face. The mouth was rendered with great realism, to reveal a line of well defined teeth, and provide the face with a lively expression. The long nose and rectangular ears imbue the mask with a symmetry and authority that convey Olmec aesthetic ideals. Strength and stoicism in a rather genderless form are seen again and again in Olmec high status art. The two holes in the ear lobes suggest the inclusion of jewelry and the single incisions across the bridge of the nose may represent a facial tattoo. This masterpiece of stonework was made without the use of any metal or mechanized tools and must have consumed many hours in the life of a craftsperson.

Sources: Taube (2004)

Mask
Olmec (Gulf Coast, Mexico)
ca. 1500-400 BCE
Jade
4 x 3 5/8 x 1"
Gift of The Rubin - Ladd Foundation, 2007.4.18

Olmec lapidary artists used a combination of stone tools with abrasive materials in order to create delicate but expressive jade masks such as this example. Natural variations in the dark green stone have been skillfully incorporated in the facial features and the narrow eyes contrast sharply with a long nose and thick lips. As in most of these masks, the mouth is open to reveal a row of teeth. Small cavities in the pupils and at the corners of the mouth may have held inlays. Both the size and the stylized traits of this mask point to a commemorative or ritual function. The material used and the sophisticated technique employed in its creation indicate this mask was a luxury item, suitable for inclusion in a rich burial or in a ritual offering.

Sources: Taube (2004)

Mask
Olmec (Gulf Coast, Mexico)
ca. 1500-400 BCE
Greenstone
4 7/8 x 4 3/8 x 3"
Gift of Mr. and Mrs. Barry Fitzmorris, 2007.52.6

Greenstone of all types was highly prized by the people of ancient Mesoamerica, for its resemblance to young sprouts of corn that appeared after the first rains. The brilliant green color and luster of the stone from which this mask is made is perhaps its most attractive element. The facial features demonstrate a perfect balance of stylized and naturalistic characteristics. The eyes, eyebrows and ears have been rendered in a minimalistic style, with only basic incisions to suggest the contours. By contrast, the nose and mouth are depicted with great realism. The nose is rounded and the nostrils flare outward. The upper lip curls to show the teeth in the characteristic Olmec gesture. Two holes at the corners of the mouth are also typical of such masks, and have been interpreted as guides in the stone working process.

Sources: Taube (2004)

Figure
Olmec (Gulf Coast, Mexico); Izapa (Pacific Coast, Mexico)
ca. 600-300 BCE
Slate and specular hematite
17 3/4 x 6 1/4 x 5/8"
Gift of Drs. Ann and Robert Waltzer, 2008.38.15

An extraordinary example of the profound influence of Olmec art upon later peoples of Mesoamerica, this two dimensional carved slate figure shares many features of Olmec art such as the flattened head, flame eyebrows, and were-jaguar mask, yet differs from the predominantly three dimensional stone carving of the Olmecs. The late Preclassic sites of Izapa and Kaminaljuyu both were strongly influenced by Olmec iconographic themes, and provide a bridge to the emergence of Maya art styles. Images such as this one provide an excellent example of the continuity of styles and themes that linked artistic production within ancient Mesoamerican societies through time. The figure stands in a posture reminiscent of Olmec jade figurines and suggestive of a shamanic trance state in which the face and legs are in profile while the torso is frontal, a convention which influenced the later Maya style of portraiture. The individual wears a mask with the curled upper lip and downturned mouth of the were-jaguar complex. At the wrists and lower legs the figure wears protective pads and the knotted cords at the ankles and waist have associations with bloodletting and self-sacrifice. The lines on arms and legs indicate tattoos or body scarification. Although a highly unusual piece, all the iconographic evidence supports an interpretation that this figure portrays a supernatural deity or ritual specialist in the midst of spirit possession.

Sources: Matos (2003), Miller (2006)

Toad
Olmec (Gulf Coast, Mexico); Izapa (Pacific Coast, Mexico)
ca. 800-300 BCE
Basalt and shell
5 x 10 3/4 x 7 3/8"
Gift of Mr. and Mrs. Barry Fitzmorris, 2007.52.5

Avid observers of their natural environment, ancient Mesoamerican artists attached great symbolic meaning to animals according to the main behavioral characteristics of each creature. The long life span and process of skin regeneration of the toad led to its identification with longevity and the fertility of the earth. The species most commonly represented is *Bufo marinus*, which was abundant in the tropical environment of the Gulf coast lowlands. This beautiful stone sculpture has been carved in basalt and has shell inlays in the eyes and along the body. The head is upright and two arched eyebrows accentuate the circular shell eyes. The nostrils are marked by two minute orifices drilled into the stone, and a long curving line indicates the mouth. The back of the animal is decorated with a curvilinear motif and more shell. The lower limbs include a spiral motif delicately incised into the stone. As symbols of the regeneration of the earth, these animals appear in the art of Mesoamerica from ancient times into the modern period.

Sources: Furst (1981)

Mask
Olmec (Gulf Coast, Mexico)
ca. 1500-400 BCE
Greenstone
3 7/8 x 4 x 2 5/8"
Gift of Mr. and Mrs. Barry Fitzmorris, 2006.36.8

Olmec stone masks are abundant in the archaeological record, and are often found in burials and offerings. The specific function of these masks is unclear, but it is unlikely they were made to be worn as most of them have no eye or nostril holes and they are usually smaller than an average human face. This mask definitely departs from a naturalistic depiction of human characteristics. The upper part shows a variation of the typical Olmec cleft forehead. Two depressed areas indicate the eye sockets. The nose is short and wide with open nostrils. The large gaping mouth shows the toothless gums and the tongue. The exaggerated emphasis on the mouth suggests a strong symbolic significance, perhaps a representation of a cave as entrance to the underworld. The iconography on this mask suggests the Olmec "avian jaguar" motif, a combination of animal attributes that pertain to diverse natural realms.

Sources: Taube (2004), *PAUM* (1995)

Figure
Olmec (Gulf Coast, Mexico)
ca. 1500-400 BCE
Stone
4 3/4 x 1 3/4 x 1 1/8"
Gift of Dr. and Mrs. Allan A. Kaplan, 90.0114

A highly polished surface, elongated head, and an abstracted rendering of facial features are all elements that identify Olmec stone sculptures as depictions of supernatural characters. This stone figurine has the typical slender shape with elongated limbs and head. Facial features are reduced to basic elements, but special emphasis was given to the mouth. At the ends of both arms linear incisions indicate fingers and an incised line around the waist serves as a minimalistic suggestion of clothing. The figure lacks any depiction of genitalia, a common trait in Olmec art. Traces of red hematite can be seen on the surface of the dark serpentine stone.

Sources: *LAM* (1990), Tate (1995)

Figure
Olmec (Gulf Coast, Mexico)
ca. 1500-400 BCE
Stone
8 3/4 x 3 5/8 x 2"
Gift of Mr. and Mrs. Barry Fitzmorris, 2005.29.4

This Olmec stone figurine follows the tradition of combining realistic and abstract elements in the depiction of human forms. Slightly more naturalistic than other examples in this exhibition, with hints of musculature and better defined hands and feet, this image nevertheless adheres to strict Olmec conventions. An elongated head and slender body are enlivened with a detailed face. A pair of circular incisions suggests the presence of inlays for the eyes. The nose is long and imposing, providing the figure with a severe expression. The mouth has thick lips which curl in a gnarled gesture common in Olmec representations. As with other stone figurines and masks, the ears are pierced, perhaps to attach jewelry. This figure exemplifies the excellent stone carving technique of Olmec artists, who used stone tools and fiber saws to achieve delicate, highly polished effects.

Sources: *PUAM* (1995)

Baby Figure
Olmec (Gulf Coast, Mexico)
ca. 1500-400 BCE
Ceramic
10 1/8 x 8 1/2 x 4 1/2"
Museum purchase, 88.0013

Hollow "baby" figures are common in Olmec ceramics and represent ageless and genderless figures possessing supernatural powers. This beautiful example shows the typical iconographic conventions. The figure is seated with extended arms and open legs. The face is emotionless although a certain gravity is transmitted. The figure lacks any garments or ornaments with the only exception being a cap that covers the head. The figure is covered in white slip paint and traces of red pigment are still visible in some parts of the body. The skull cap is covered in bitumen. With variation in postures and expressions along with a lack of adequate provenience for most of the figures, it is difficult to identify the specific function or significance of the hollow baby figures. Some interpretations suggest they are purely symbolic images, while others see them as portrayals of important individuals within Olmec society. It is undeniable that the early artists who produced these images possessed a keen eye for realistic portrayal of the human form as well as a sophisticated clay modeling technique.

Sources: *LAM* (1990), *PUAM* (1995)

Maya

MAYA
Classic Period, 200-900 CE

Maya civilization flourished in the mountains and especially the lowlands of southern Mexico, Belize, Guatemala, El Salvador and western Honduras. Well adapted to the tropics, the Classic Maya are known for sprawling cities of funerary pyramids and palaces connected by raised roads, a distinctive art style, and a tradition of literacy that was unmatched elsewhere in the ancient New World. Many visitors are familiar with the impressive cities of Tikal, Copan, Chichen Itza, and Calakmul, but many hundreds of Classic Maya cities remain unexcavated today.

Maya society was ruled by competing dynasties of semi-divine royalty who performed rituals of deity impersonation for the greater population. Ancestral veneration was central to the ability of dynasties to maintain political power, and the elaborate tombs of kings and queens were often re-entered for rituals of commemoration. The Maize Deity symbolized the ability of elites to ensure the return of the most important food crop, and was often depicted in art and costume. Maya elites developed a fully functional writing system to record dynastic history and significant dates in the calendar system using stone inscriptions and painted texts.

A rich economy based on trade and contact with the other cultures of ancient Mesoamerica led to distinct regional traditions within the millions of people who lived in the Maya area. The production of art was tightly controlled by ruling families who established workshops within their palaces. Most of the objects included in this exhibition were made at the order of a king or queen. Art was frequently exchanged between visiting dignitaries, given in offering to the gods or ancestors, and worn or used to display royal status.

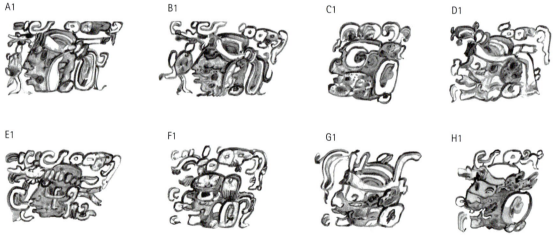

Bowl with Eight Portrait Glyphs
Maya (Guatemala)
ca. 600-900 CE
Ceramic
3 ½ x 9 ⅜"
Gift of Dr. and Mrs. Allan A. Kaplan, 85.0071

This beautifully painted bowl is decorated with the head variant or portrait glyphs of eight of the major deities of the Classic Maya pantheon. Included are the Hero Twins, as well as a pair of gods known as Jaguar Paddler and Stingray Paddler, who were responsible for paddling a canoe containing the Maize Deity from the Underworld to the place of his rebirth. The iconography on this bowl suggests that it was part of the funerary goods of a person of high status, made to accompany him or her in their journey after death.

Source: *BD* (1990)

Toad Effigy Jar
Maya (El Salvador)
ca. 600-900 CE
Ceramic
5 x 5"
Gift of Dr. and Mrs. Allan A. Kaplan, 81.0352

This vessel in the form of the *Bufo marinus* toad, may have been an elaborate container used in the administration of hallucinogenic enemas among the Maya elite. The circular symbols on the sides are associated with enema pots and the glands of the *Bufo* toad secrete a toxin that is known to have been used by the ancient Maya to produce visions. The lords and jaguar portrayed around the rim underscore the importance of this ceremony and this vessel.

Sources: *LAM* (2006), *BD* (1990)

Spouted Jar
Maya-related (El Salvador)
ca. 300 BCE – 400 CE
Ceramic
9 1/8 x 10 x 9 5/8"
Gift of Enrico Varisco in memory of Roberto Varisco, 2003.63.64

Large spouted jars such as this one have been found to contain the residue of a frothy chocolate drink, used in feasts and ceremonies. A batten was used to stir and froth the chocolate which was poured from the spout in a long stream to even further aerate the drink. The wax resist decoration of this jar indicates it is from the Usulutan area of eastern El Salvador/western Honduras.

Spouted Jar
Lenca (El Salvador or Honduras)
ca. 300 BCE-400 CE
Ceramic
7 ½ x 10 ¼ x 9 ⅛"
Gift of Jose Roberto Rivas, Donaldo Vela and Ricardo Monterrosa, 86.0094

The Lenca people lived in eastern El Salvador and central-western Honduras and were independent of the Maya city-states around them. They lived in advanced chiefdoms and traded with many cultural groups from Mesoamerica. Large spouted jars such as this one have been found to contain the residue of a frothy chocolate drink, used in feasts and ceremonies. This chocolate vessel is decorated with a human head.

Spouted Jar
Lenca (El Salvador or Honduras)
ca. 300 BCE-400 CE
Ceramic
6 ¾ x 9 ⅜ x 8 ⅝"
Gift of Jose Roberto Rivas, Donaldo Vela and Ricardo Monterrosa, 86.0095

The Lenca people of El Salvador and central-western Honduras were highly influenced by the Maya city-states around them. Throughout Mesoamerica people practiced feasting as a means of social negotiation, and large spouted jars such as this one have been found to contain the residue of a spicy chocolate drink, used in feasts and ceremonies.

Pendant
Maya (Guatemala)
ca. 600-900 CE
Jade
1 5/8 x 7/8 x 1/4"
Gift of Dr. And Mrs. Allan A. Kaplan, 79.018.010

This lovely jade pendant is carved in the form of a volute or scroll which was an important symbol in Maya iconography. It can represent the wind or movement of water, as well as the words and exhalations of important nobles.

Carved Plaque
Maya (Guatemala)
ca. 600-900 CE
Greenstone
1 7/8 x 1 5/8 x 3/8"
Gift of The Institute for Maya Studies, 80.0057

This portrait of a high ranking ruler with large earflares may have been incomplete as it shows very little sign of wear. Greenstone and jade jewels such as this were believed to hold the regenerative powers of maize and were worn by elites to indicate their rank.

Source: *BD* (1990)

Finger Ring
Maya (Guatemala)
ca. 600-900 CE
Shell
3/8 x 1 x 7/8"
Gift of Dr. and Mrs. Allan A. Kaplan, 80.0101

Shell jewelry was an important component of royal costume, both for the decorative aspect but also because of the economic and ideological significance of the sea within Classic Maya society. Finger rings are extremely rare and this example was likely the work of a master craftsperson. It is carved with the portrait of a ruler wearing an elaborate headdress and decorated with 5 inlaid jewels, perhaps of jade or hematite.

Bead
Maya (Guatemala)
ca. 600-900 CE
Jade
5/8 x 3/4 x 3/4"
Gift of Dr. and Mrs. David Light, 83.0027

Jade beads were often carved in the form of animals that held particular significance to Maya society. This bead depicts a monkey, an animal revered for its intelligence and cunning.

Pendants
Maya (Guatemala)
ca. 600-900 CE
Jade
1 ⁵/₈ x ³/₈ x ¹/₈"
Gift of Dr. and Mrs. David Light, 83.0031 & 83.0032

This perfectly matched set of pendants combine the inherent power of jade, a substance that the Maya believed to convey life force, with the dominance represented by a jaguar's claw. They are an excellent example of the way the natural world was appropriated as a metaphor for royal power by Maya kings and queens.

Carved Plaque
Maya (Guatemala)
ca. 600-900 CE
Jade
2 x 1 ⁵/₈ x ⁵/₈"
Gift of Dr. and Mrs. David Light, 86.0189

This pendant shows a ruler wearing a high status headdress with scrolls that may represent bright green quetzal feathers and jade ear flares. Portraits such as these were worn by elite members of society to indicate their privileged status.

Source: *BD* (1990)

Carved Plaque
Maya (Guatemala)
ca. 600-900 CE
Jade
2 ½ x 1 ½"
Gift of Dr. and Mrs. David Light, 86.0190

This lovely jade plaque shows the profile of a warrior wearing an elaborate headdress in the form of a feathered serpent. Small jade jewels such as this were worn by high ranking members of Maya society to indicate their royal status.

Source: *BD* (1990)

Pendant
Maya (Guatemala)
ca. 600-900 CE
Jade
2 ⁷⁄₈ x 1 ½ x 1 ¼"
Gift of Dr. and Mrs. David Light, 86.0191

This pendant shows a ruler wearing a high status headdress with a bird beak and feathers, jade ear flares, and a thick jade necklace. Portraits such as these were worn by elite members of society to indicate their privileged status.

Pendant
Maya (Guatemala)
ca. 600-900 CE
Jade
1 3/4 x 7/8 x 5/8"
Gift of Enrico Varisco in memory of Roberto Varisco, 2003.63.4

The tall tonsured hair of this figure suggests the young, handsome Maize Deity. Jade pendants are common at Maya archaeological sites and were probably worn by a large percentage of the ancient population.

Pendant
Maya (Guatemala)
ca. 600-900 CE
Jade
3 x 3/4 x 3/8"
Gift of Enrico Varisco in memory of Roberto Varisco, 2003.63.80

This jade pendant in the form of a jaguar claw may have been worn by a ruler whose royal family carried the jaguar as their animal companion spirit.

Pendant
Maya (Honduras)
ca. 600-900 CE
Jade
2 3/8 x 1/2"
Gift of Sylvia Coppersmith in memory of Dora Coppersmith, S86.0049

Jade was the most precious material known to the ancient Maya, more valuable than gold or copper. The range of greenish blue colors found in this mineral reminded the Maya of young sprouts of corn, the staple on which the entire civilization was built. Rulers, elites, and even wealthy commoners wore jade whenever possible. This bead was most likely worn over the heart.

Bead
Maya (Honduras)
ca. 600-900 CE
Jade
3/4 x 1 x 5/8"
Gift of Sylvia Coppersmith in memory of Dora Coppersmith, 86.0057

Rabbits were seen as clever and useful creatures by the ancient Maya, who sometimes depicted the highly trained courtly scribe as a rabbit. Powerful individuals sometimes had what we might consider today modest animals as their spirit companions, including the famous Maya king from Honduras, 18 Rabbit. This lovely bead is made of a very light colored jade.

Mirror
Maya (Honduras)
ca. 600-900 CE
Slate and pyrite
³/₈ x 4 ⁵/₈"
Gift of Sylvia Coppersmith in memory of Dora Coppersmith, 86.0060

Maya craftsmen were able to polish small mosaic pieces of pyrite to a high sheen and by piecing them together, create a reflective mirror. Mirrors were part of many ceremonies and may have been a tool for royal members of society to communicate with their ancestors. Worn as a pendant over the chest of a ruler, most of the pyrite is still adhered to the slate backing of this large mirror.

Source: Helmke (2006)

Necklace
Maya (Yucatan, Mexico)
ca. 600-900 CE
Shell
6 ¾ x 3 ¼ x 1 ½"
Gift of Sylvia Coppersmith in memory of Dora Coppersmith, 86.0059

Shells were a valuable source of durable material for tools and ornaments. This necklace made of drilled shell beads and a single conch shell is an unusual example. The conch shell has inscribed designs reminiscent of a single glyph block. Children are often found interred with shell ornaments and the dimensions of this necklace suggest it may have been made for a child.

Stamp
Maya (Guatemala)
ca. 600-900 CE
Ceramic
3 x 2 ⁵/₈ x 1 ½"
Gift of The Institute of Maya Studies, 80.0024

Ceramic stamps were used for many purposes, such as decorating plain cotton cloth or applying body paint. This stamp in the image of a jaguar's paw, might have literally marked the wearer with the royal power of this important cat.

Paint Pot
Maya (El Salvador)
ca. 600-900 CE
Ceramic
1 ⁵/₈ x 1 ⁷/₈ x 2 ¼"
Gift of Dr. and Mrs. Allan A. Kaplan, 81.0351

This very small pot was used to hold pigment, perhaps for decorating a Maya ceramic vase, bark book, or for facial and body tattoos. It is decorated with a bearded face which may reference the Sun god Kinich Ahau, or one of the *pahuatuns*, the four old gods of the earth.

Ballgame Yoke
Maya (Mexico)
ca. 300-600 CE
Granite
4 ½ x 13 ¾ x 15 ¾"
Gift of The Rubin-Ladd Foundation, 2008.39.11

One of the preeminent masculine rituals for elite Maya men of the Classic period was the ballgame. Royal men are shown wearing stone yokes on painted Maya ceramics but scholars disagree on whether the heavy ornaments were actually worn during play, or were for display before and after the game. This example is carved in an early style and shows a crouching jaguar with open maw.

Pendants
Maya (Honduras)
ca. 600-900 CE
Greenstone
⅛ x 3 x 2 ⅞"
Gift of Mr. and Mrs. Robert Stoetzer, 91.0374.01 & 91.0374.02

This matching set of greenstone ornaments may have been part of the royal regalia or costume worn by a high ranking ruler to convey his or her status. All forms of greenstone, not just jade, were highly valued and worn as talismans of life force. This matching set has tiny holes for suspension and is decorated with a star symbol, often a representation of success in war.

Flask
Maya (Guatemala)
ca. 600-900 CE
Ceramic
2 ½ x 1 ⅝ x 1 ¼"
Gift of The Institute of Maya Studies, 80.0032

Ceramic mold made flasks such as this one have recently been identified as receptacles for powdered tobacco and other medicinal herbs. Long known as poison bottles, residue analysis and decipherment of the glyphic captions on many flasks suggest they were closely associated with God L, the old shaman and personification of tobacco. This rectangular architectural example has the sloping roof and thatch of a miniature house, and the individual portrayed within may be a ruler or God L himself. The other three sides carry a glyphic inscription.

Source: Carlson (2007)

Flask
Maya (Guatemala)
ca. 600-900 CE
Ceramic
3 x 1 ⅞ x 1 ⅛"
Gift of Mr. and Mrs. Robert Stoetzer, 86.0034

The sloping roof, thatch, and dimensions of a traditional Maya house can be seen in this rectangular architectural example of a Maya tobacco flask. This mold made example is decorated with serpent masks on both sides, perhaps as an indication that the mind altering state conveyed from tobacco ingestion facilitated communion with powerful ancestors, often portrayed as serpents in Maya art.

Source: Carlson (2007)

Flask
Maya (Guatemala)
ca. 600-900 CE
Ceramic with specular hematite
2 ¼ x 1 ¾ x 1 ⅜"
Gift of Dr. and Mrs. Allan A. Kaplan, 86.0186

This tiny mold made flask may have originally held the deep red pigment preserved on the outer surface. Specular hematite and other red minerals such as cinnabar, were precious offerings used by the ancient Maya in burials and caches. This vessel is decorated with the fat face god, who may be a variant of the *pahuatuns*, or earth deities responsible for holding up the sky.

Source: Carlson (2007)

Eccentric Flint
Maya (Belize)
ca. 600-900 CE
Flint
6 x 7 x ⅝"
Museum purchase through 35th Anniversary Funds, 85.0078

Three faces or profiles can be seen in this exceptional example of flint knapping. Master artisans crafted objects such as these, called "eccentrics" because each one is unique, from chert and flint found in the Maya Mountains. These objects were mounted on a wooden staff and carried in royal processions, they were never meant to be used like other flint tools such as projectile points. Later they were deposited in royal tombs and caches.

Press Mold
Maya (Guatemala)
ca. 700-1000 CE
Ceramic
4 3/8 x 3 5/8 x 3"
Gift of Enrico Varisco in memory of Roberto Varisco, 2003.63.91

Many Maya ceramic pieces were individually hand crafted but molds became more popular later in the Classic period when demand for incense burners and figurines increased. Some of the incense burners included in this exhibition have faces that were mold made and hand modeled bodies, showing that mold made pieces were often re-touched by hand to yield a unique piece without loosing the efficiency of mass production. This mold was used to produce a smiling face with an ornate headdress. The exterior of the mold is decorated with a standing lord.

Whistle
Maya (Honduras)
ca. 600-900 CE
Ceramic
1 x 2 3/4 x 1 5/8"
Gift of Sylvia Coppersmith in memory of Lelia C. Rosen, 84.0152

This whistle takes the form of an alligator or caiman, both well known reptiles of the Central American tropics. Whistles were used in ceremonies and as toys for children.

Hieroglyphic Panel Fragment
Maya (Seibal, Petén, Guatemala)
ca. 700-800 CE
Limestone
19 ½ x 13 ½ x 2 ⅞"
Gift of an Anonymous Donor, 93.0043.04

This fragment from Tablet 3 of the hieroglyphic stairway at the site of Seibal, records a scattering event in the upper-left glyph block and the associated ceremonies performed by K'awiil Chan K'inich, *ch'ul ajaw* (holy lord) of Dos Pilas, who celebrated this ritual at the site of Seibal on May 30, 746 (7 Etz'nab 16 Xul in the Maya calendar). According to other textual sources, Dos Pilas won a decisive victory over Seibal approximately ten years earlier and this stairway commemorated the vassal status of Seibal. K'awiil Chan K'inich was named for one of the principal Maya deities, in this case K'awiil, the god of royal bloodlines. Parts of this text were removed from the stairway in antiquity and surviving elements were moved to the archaeological camp at the turn of the 20th century. Sadly many of these have now disappeared. Maya hieroglyphic writing was one of the most sophisticated notational systems of the ancient world.

Sources: *LAM* (2006)

Lidded Vessel
Maya (Guatemala)
ca. 600-900 CE
Ceramic and specular hematite
9 ⅞ x 6 ¾"
Gift of Mr. and Mrs. Robert Stoetzer, 94.0054.02

With this beautiful vessel we see another example of how the boundaries between the animal and human worlds were permeable in ancient Maya art. Commissioned for a funerary assemblage, the lid of this tripod vase is decorated with a finely modeled head that displays both jaguar and human characteristics. Powerful animal companion spirits accompanied the dead on their journey to the Underworld and perhaps this vessel held an offering related to such a passage.

Incense Burner
Maya (Guatemala)
ca. 600-900 CE
Ceramic
14 ½ x 10 x 6"
Museum purchase through 1987 Acquisition Funds, 85.0154

An extraordinary two piece incense burner, this figurine depicts the dancing ritual clowns that were priests of God N, the aged earth deity. Throughout Mesoamerica ritual clowning was used to mark transitional periods such as the end of the calendar year, and ritual clowns held key roles in the performance of ceremonies meant to resolve the potential chaos that accompanies beginnings and endings. One side of the figure wears a woven or netted cap with rolled ends, the characteristic cloth headdress of God N while the other side has the tonsured hair characteristic of the personified *pa* glyph in Maya art which represents a ritual clown with monkey aspects. The individual wears a long loincloth that reveals both legs, anklets, and knots of rope on both arms to signify the ritual status of the costume. A goggle eyed mask of coarse woven cloth covers her or his face and a dance rattle is held in the right hand. Two part effigy vessels of dancing ritual clowns have been found at the Early Classic site of Kaminaljuyu in modern day Guatemala and it is likely this figurine dates to the same period.

Source: Taube (1989)

Incense Burner
Maya (Guatemala)
ca. 1200-1500 CE
Ceramic
2 5/8 x 11 1/8 x 5 3/4"
Gift of Dr. and Mrs. Allan A. Kaplan, 79.018.016

Resin incense gathered from the tropical forest was one of the most precious offerings in Maya religion. During the Postclassic period, ladles such as this one, were used to carry burning incense in processions and other rituals. The handles of certain important tools, such as weaving picks, paint brushes, and incense ladles were decorated with human hands, in order to emphasize the responsibility of their owners to use them correctly. The end of this object is half human hand and half jaguar paw.

Tripod Bowl
Maya-related (Ulúa Valley, Honduras)
ca. 650-750 CE
Marble
6 x 9 5/8"
Museum purchase, 87.0002

Elaborate carved marble bowls such as this one were made in a single valley of modern day Honduras and traded throughout the Classic Maya world. They were highly valued for the semi-translucent quality of the marble that warmed to the touch. This example has handles made in the form of a bat, an animal with close ties to both the supernatural arena of caves, believed to be entrances to the Underworld, as well as royal dynasties at sites such as Copan. Bats also thrive in cacao, or chocolate groves, another very important trade items from this part of Honduras. The volutes, or swirls around the body of this vase may represent the movement of water or blood, but it has also been suggested they are speech scrolls or the exhalation required for speech. The upper and lower borders are meant to resemble the scales of a lizard or snake.

Sources: *LAM* (2006), Luke (2002), *BD* (1990)

Stela
Maya (Campeche, Mexico)
ca. 600-900 CE
Limestone
46 x 18 x 3
Museum purchase and partial gift of Mary Cassard, 89.0006

This monumental sculpture was erected to commemorate the achievements of the royal individual, probably a king or secondary lord, depicted on the front of the stela. The short hieroglyphic text on the upper left hand side of the monument, now largely eroded, recorded his name and accomplishments. The elaborate headdress and jade jewels he wears indicate his high status. He holds his hands in a posture consistent with an incense scattering ritual, a form of offering to spirits or ancestors that royal Maya individuals performed on behalf of their lineage and city-state. Previous commentators have suggested that this lord is letting blood from his genitals but this important ritual act is rarely portrayed in stone portraiture.

Sources: *LAM* (2006), *BD* (1990)

Urn
Maya (Guatemala)
ca. 300-600 CE
Ceramic
16 1/4 x 11 5/8 x 12 7/8"
Museum purchase, 90.0017

The base of this elaborate urn has been modeled with the face of G-3, or Kinich Ahau, the sun-eyed lord. Kinich Ahau personified the Sun on its journey through the Underworld, and in this sense is often conflated with the Jaguar God of the Underworld. Large urns such as this one were made as burial offerings and were interred in tombs. Uneven weathering of these two pieces may account for the difference in color, or they may have originally come from two separate vessels.

Source: *BD* (1990)

Funerary Urn
Maya (Highlands (K'iche), Guatemala)
ca. 700-900 CE
Ceramic
18 3/8 x 17 3/4 x 17 1/4"
Gift of Mr. and Mrs. Robert Stoetzer, 91.0376

Large ceramic urns such as this one have rarely been excavated in context so their exact function is debated. They are believed to be associated with tombs and other funerary offerings, and in some cases held the remains of a bundled burial. In other cases they may have been filled with resin incense that was offered to the gods during a funerary ritual. On this example we see an animated jaguar depicted in the posture of sacrifice bordered by two human long bones. This may be a reference to the death of the royal person who commissioned this urn.

Incense Burner Lid
Maya (Guatemala)
ca. 600-900 CE
Ceramic
9 5/8 x 4 3/4 x 4 3/8"
Gift of The Institute of Maya Studies, 80.0026

There were many different types of incense burners in Classic Maya society, perhaps as a result of the many different types of resin incense available in the Maya tropics. This interesting piece is the lid to a large vessel that would have allowed billowing clouds of smoke to swirl up and around the image of a woman holding an infant deer. Maya women allowed deer to graze upon their gardens and may have even planted small plots of corn just for these semi-domesticated animals. Deer were economically important and provided one of the few sources of animal protein in the Classic Maya diet.

Incense Burner Lid
Maya (Guatemala)
ca. 600-900 CE
Ceramic
9 5/8 x 4 1/2 x 4"
Gift of Dr. and Mrs. Allan A. Kaplan, 80.0125

This representation of a female deity with jaguar characteristics is the mold-made lid to a larger vessel that would have allowed billowing clouds of smoke to swirl up and around the deity image. The bare breasts of this goddess are visible, as are her facial tattoos and elaborate ear ornaments. The female creator deity Chak Chel is sometimes shown with clawed hands and feet to indicate her connection with this fierce animal. It is thought that the jaguar may have been one of her animal alter egos.

Bowl
Maya (Guatemala)
ca. 900-1100 CE
Ceramic
6 1/8 x 6 1/8"
Gift of The Institute for Maya Studies, 80.0054

This elegant vessel is decorated with a dancing monkey, probably a spider monkey *(Ateles geoffroyi)* common in the rainforest environments of Guatemala, Belize and Mexico. The ancient Maya saw the monkey as the patron god of writing and they were revered for their intelligence. Spider monkeys in particular were seen as representative of fertility and sensuality. This vessel may have been made to serve guests at a high status feast.

Source: *BD* (1990)

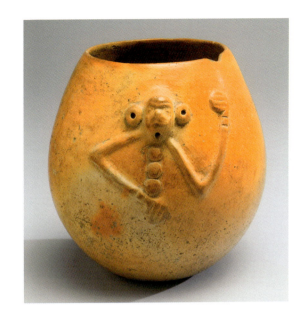

Turtle Effigy Jar
Maya (El Salvador)
ca. 600-900 CE
Ceramic
1 3/4 x 3 x 2 3/8"
Gift of The Institute for Maya Studies, 80.0038

Small jars like this one were used to hold pigments for painting Maya ceramics, bark books, or perhaps for cosmetics. This turtle jar has been decorated with a lead based slip and fired at a very high temperature. This technique travelled from central Mexico down the Pacific coast. Many Mesoamerican people believed the world rested on the back of a land turtle.

Figurine
Maya (Campeche, Mexico)
ca. 600-900 CE
Ceramic
9 1/8 x 3 1/4 x 2 1/4
Gift of Mr. and Mrs. Robert Stoetzer, 86.0033

This detailed figurine depicts a warrior dressed for battle. The individual wears a relatively simple protective head cover, quilted cotton armor and carries a large wooden shield. His high status is indicated by the large jade portrait head he wears on his chest as well as his large earflares. Intricate figurines such as this one were often found on the Maya funerary island of Jaina and this object may have been made to commemorate the accomplishments of a revered ancestor.

Source: *BD* (1990)

Figurine
Maya (Campeche, Mexico)
ca. 600-900 CE
ceramic, red, white, blue pigment
7 1/8 x 3 3/4
Gift of Dr. and Mrs. Allan A. Kaplan, 85.0067

The island of Jaina, off the coast of Campeche in the Yucatan peninsula, is well known for the beautiful and realistic ceramic portraits of elite Maya women and men known to have come from burials on the island. Jaina may have been a symbolic portal to the otherworld, and only select high status individuals were allowed to be interred there. This lovely figurine is a portrait of a high status woman, perhaps a queen. The unbroken profile and almond shaped eyes are illustrative of Classic Maya ideals of female beauty. Her elaborate floor length dress, or Maya *huipil*, is embellished with embroidery and paint, and her hair has been arranged in a sophisticated fashion. She wears jade jewels and carries a small rattle. This mold made figurine is itself a rattle, with small ceramic balls inside that through their sound, indicated that the figurine was alive. Similarities in modeling suggest connections to figurines of central Veracruz.

Sources: *LAM* (2006), *BD* (1990)

Grinding Stone
Maya (Honduras)
ca. 600-900 CE
Basalt
7 ½ x 14 ⅛ x 20 ¼"
Gift of Sylvia Coppersmith in memory of Dora Coppersmith, 86.0083

Ornate grinding stones were made throughout ancient Mesoamerica and are still used today for ceremonial purposes, although the mechanized *molino* has replaced these tools for daily use. A high ranking person might have had multiple metates in their household in ancient times, each with a different decoration. This example has the head of a feathered serpent, important throughout ancient Mesoamerica, as a decorative element.

Vase
Maya (Guatemala)
ca. 600-900 CE
Ceramic
5 ⅞ x 4 ¼
Gift of an Anonymous Donor, 93.0043.03

This colorful vase depicts two lords engaged in palace negotiations. Each leans in to speak with the other, and a block of unfinished glyphs separate the two, indicating they are speaking. Each figure wears the daily cotton loincloth typical of royal Maya lords and an elaborate headdress to indicate their high rank. Bright red, blue and yellow pigments were applied to a thin layer of stucco on this ceramic vase, and it is rare to find such stucco so well preserved.

Sources: *LAM* (2006)

Cylinder Vase
Maya (Guatemala)
ca. 650–850 CE
Ceramic
7 x 6 ⅛"
Museum purchase through the Thea Katzenstein Art Acquisition Endowment Fund, 2009.26

A special acquisition for *The Jaguar's Spots* exhibition, this codex style vase shows an older lord with headdress and axe characteristic of the rain god Chahk with two attendants behind him. The attendants wear the sarong and tonsured hair of palace scribes and may be in attendance at a ceremony in order to commemorate the performance of this rite. Before the lord are three figures dressed as hunters and a central figure embodying the Maize Deity. Five glyphic captions frame the actors. The iconography, texts and possible provenance of this vase are fully discussed in chapter six.

Text 1	Text 2	Text 3	Text 4	
A1–A3	B1–B3	C1, D1, E1	F1–F7	G1–G6

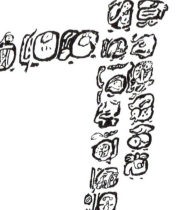

Tripod Vase
Maya-related (Honduras)
ca. 600-900 CE
Ceramic
8 3/8 x 6 5/8"
Gift of Mr. and Mrs. Robert Stoetzer, 91.0368

Tall tripod vases such as this one were often made to hold liquid offerings placed in the tomb or burial of a wealthy person. This vase is decorated with painted images of rulers dressed in an elaborate feather headdress. The top and bottom borders contain large bats with supernatural characteristics, perhaps an indication that the individuals are inside a cave or the Underworld. The colors of this vase indicate it fits within the Ulua-Yojoa polychrome tradition.

Jar
Maya (Honduras)
ca. 700-1200 CE
Ceramic
11 1/4 x 7 1/8 x 9"
Gift of David M. Stoetzer, 2005.51.2

The god of wind, known as Ehecatl in central Mexico, may be depicted on this later vase from Honduras. The power of wind, breath and speech were closely linked in ancient Mesoamerica and this god literally breathed life into the human race. The dual loop handles on this vase allowed for suspension and the rope across the forehead of the deity suggests a tumpline, the most common means by which a heavy burden of cargo was carried in ancient times.

Bowl
Maya-related (Honduras)
ca. 600-900 CE
Ceramic
4 x 6 7/8"
Gift of Seymour Rosenberg, 81.0226

Three elaborate feathered serpent heads decorate this polychrome bowl. The feathered serpent was an important icon throughout ancient Mesoamerica and represented the gods of wind and merchants. Worship of this deity was spread from central Mexico through Honduras at the time of European contact. The vibrant red and orange of this bowl indicate it is likely part of the Ulua-Yojoa polychrome tradition of central Honduras.

Source: Healy (1984)

Urn
Maya (Guatemala)
ca. 600-900 CE
Ceramic
13 x 18 5/8 x 15"
Gift of Mr. and Mrs. Robert Stoetzer, 94.0054.01

Like many incense burners and urns from the Maya area, spikes protrude from this piece just as they do on the trunk of an immature ceiba *(Ceiba pentandra)* tree, the world tree in Maya cosmology. This piece also portrays the Mesoamerican understanding of life and death—on one side of the vessel is a death mask, on the other is a human or god face. A knotted rope connects the two. The imagery suggests the vessel was made or used in rituals that connected the Underworld of death with the upper world of the living.

Vessel Lid
Maya (Guatemala)
ca. 600-900 CE
Ceramic
1 7/8 x 6 3/4"
Gift of May Cassard, 98.0050

Plants of great economic importance were often abstracted into geometric designs on Maya ceramics and especially daily tools such as spindle whorls. This lovely bowl was made to cover a larger jar, perhaps a storage container of some type. The seven petals of this piece recall the cross section of a ripe cotton boll or squash fruit—both plants that contributed to long distance trade throughout the Maya region.

Plate
Maya (Campeche, Mexico)
ca. 600-900 CE
Ceramic
3 1/2 x 15 3/8"
Gift of Mr. and Mrs. Robert Stoetzer, 86.0199

Large plates such as this one were made to hold tamales and other sacred foods for feasts and funerary offerings. The image on this plate of a masked man wearing a full jaguar pelt and carrying a staff or spear suggests a ruler or court dancer in full high status regalia. The loose lines of the figural art on this piece are characteristic of polychrome pottery from Campeche.

Sources: *BD* (1990)

Lidded Vessel
Maya (Campeche, Mexico)
ca. 300-600 CE
Ceramic
11 ¼ x 13 ⅞"
Gift of Dr. and Mrs. Allan A. Kaplan, 86.0188

An Early Classic Maya polychrome vessel decorated with a jaguar finial cover, this elaborate piece of art was likely made as a tomb or burial offering. One the preeminent symbols of royal authority, the jaguar was modeled into a handle while the remainder of the vessel was painted with a dense concentration of scrolls and geometric designs. Similar vessels are well known from the important Maya city-state of Calakmul, in modern Campeche, Mexico.

Face
Maya (Yucatan, Mexico)
ca. 900-1400 CE
Ceramic
4 7/8 x 4 7/8 x 2 5/8"
Gift of Enrico Varisco in memory of Roberto Varisco, 2003.63.1

This fragment of a human head was likely made to adorn the exterior of a large incense burner or effigy vessel. This face shows a depiction of facial tattooing or scarification on the right side, as well as facial painting on the left A distinctive pigment known as 'Maya Blue' covers the headdress.

Bowl
Maya (Guatemala)
ca. 600-900 CE
Ceramic
5 1/8 x 7 5/8"
Gift of Seymour Rosenberg, 81.0223

This elegant bowl shows three nearly identical portraits of a ruler in a palace setting; only the hand gestures of the individual vary. Each is framed by three glyph bands that are decorative rather than literate. Known as 'pseudoglyphs" these elements convey to us that the artist or individual who commissioned the bowl desired to convey literacy and the knowledge of writing, even though it was out of reach. A bowl such as this would have made a fine gift to exchange with a visiting dignitary or official.

Bowl
Maya (Campeche, Mexico)
ca. 600-900 CE
Ceramic
5 1/8 x 6 1/2"
Gift of Seymour Rosenberg, 81.0224

The favorite colors for Maya ceramic artists are used to set off an image of a portly jaguar. Jaguars appear frequently in Maya art as symbols of royal power and divine authority. This jaguar has a shawl or other ornamentation around his neck which may indicate he is the deity known as the Water Lily Jaguar, an important fertility god of the Classic Maya who is often shown as a huge cat who protects the members of certain royal families. Two small drill holes show this vessel was repaired in antiquity.

Sources: *LAM* (2006), *BD* (1990)

Incense Burner
Maya (Pacific coast, Guatemala)
ca. 400-650 CE
Ceramic
19 5/8 x 18 1/8 x 17 3/8"
Museum purchase through 35th Anniversary Funds, 85.0192

Large ceramic urns such as this one have rarely been excavated in context so their exact function is debated. They are believed to be associated with tombs and other funerary offerings, and in some cases were filled with resin incense that was offered to the gods during a funerary ritual. On this example we can see a high status individual, probably a priest or ruler, emerging from the mouth of a leaf nosed bat. This bat may be a protector spirit tied to the family of the individual depicted. A very similar urn is in the collection of the Museum of Fine Arts, Boston

Source: *BD* (1990)

Ballgame Yoke
Maya (Guatemala)
ca. 600-900 CE
Stone and specular hematite
4 ⁵/₈ x 13 ⁷/₈ x 16"
Gift of Mr. and Mrs. Robert Stoetzer, 2004.70.3

Maya kings and other high ranking lords played a sporting game in which they wore heavy belts, or yokes, like this one, and hit a solid rubber ball off their thighs, knees and elbows. The ballgame was played throughout Mesoamerican prehistory and ornate stone yokes are the durable remains of the ubiquity of this game. This example is decorated on both ends with the head of the young Maize Deity and may have been worn for display before or after the game, rather than as field equipment.

Vase
Maya (Yucatan, Mexico)
ca. 700-900 CE
Ceramic, specular hematite, stucco, and pigment
8 ½ x 5 ½ x 5 ⁵/₈"
Gift of Dr. and Mrs. Allan A. Kaplan, 85.0076

Tall cylindrical vessels like this were made for serving a frothy and spicy chocolate drink at royal ceremonies and feasts. The ceramic vase was originally covered in a thin layer of stucco painted a bright "Maya blue" to accentuate the glyph panels carved with an elaborated *ajaw* glyph and colored with ground specular hematite. The Maya favored the deep red of hematite for its similarity to blood, an important and precious offering.

Source: *BD* (1990)

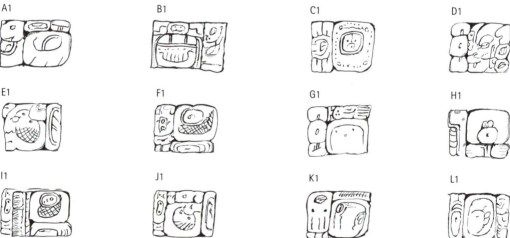

Bowl
Maya (Yucatan, Mexico)
ca. 600-900 CE
Ceramic, specular hematite
3 ½ x 8 ½"
Gift of May Cassard, 86.0210

Maya ceramic vessels are often embellished with a formulaic hieroglyphic text known as the Primary Standard Sequence. It is less common for the PSS to be present on carved ceramics, yet this unique example clearly includes the PSS text with a dedicatory statement, the type of vessel, the substance it was used for and the owner. In this example from the northern Maya lowlands, the owner of the thin walled drinking cup is described as a *sajal* or subordinate ruler as well as a *bakab*, a title that refers to the beings who hold up the sky. The base of the vessel has been carved to resemble a squash, another food sacred to the Maya.

Source: *BD* (1990)

Vase
Maya (Guatemala)
ca. 600-900 CE
Ceramic
8 x 4 ½"
Gift of Dr. and Mrs. Allan A. Kaplan, 81.0337

Tall cylinder vases such as this one were made to serve spicy chocolate drinks and have been found throughout Mesoamerica and as far north as the American Southwest. The inscribed designs on this vase are very abstract and while they contain certain phonetic elements such as *yax* (blue-green) and *na* (house), they do not appear to be decipherable. The extent of literacy in ancient Maya society is debated, but it seems clear from vases such as this one that some artists knew a few glyphs but did not have the training to construct an entire glyphic passage.

Cylinder Vase
Maya (Guatemala)
ca. 600-900 CE
Ceramic
7 ⅝ x 5"
Gift of Mr. and Mrs. Robert Stoetzer, 2004.70.2

Cylinder vases were often made to commemorate a state visit or similar official function. This vase shows a procession of secondary lords paying homage to their king, who stands on a throne with jaguar pelt decoration and wears the regalia of his office. None of the glyphs on this vase are readable, although they are positioned to suggest conversation. The final lord in the procession wears the same back rack costume as the king.

Vase
Maya (Petén, Guatemala)
ca. 600-900 CE
Ceramic
7 1/2 x 6 1/8"
Museum purchase, 89.0080

This highly detailed ceramic vase depicts a procession of high ranking lords to visit a king. The king is seated on a throne, he holds a shield and staff and wears an elaborate headdress that may associate him with the Maya rain god Chahk. The visitors all carry spears and may be receiving military instructions. Royal or high rank is indicated in those who wear jaguar pelts and animal companion headdresses. The beautiful thin black lines that outline these figures, white background, and sociopolitical subject matter suggest the vessel was made at a workshop near the site of Motul de San Jose, where Ik' style artists excelled at ceramic painting. The many small drill holes in this vessel are from efforts to repair cracks in antiquity and indicate how precious this vessel was to its owner.

Sources: *LAM* (2006), Reents-Budet (1994), *BD* (1990)

Bowl
Maya (Guatemala)
ca. 600-900 CE
Ceramic
3 1/4 x 8 1/2"
Gift of Mr. and Mrs. Robert Stoetzer, 89.0085

Two images of God K, or GII of the Palenque Triad, appear on this black and white painted bowl. God K is a common image on Maya ceramics and symbolizes the bounty that comes with royal dynastic power, as well as lightning, flint and other natural forces that provide access to power. God K, Kawil, frequently appears on black and white codex style vessels from the area around Nakbe, in the Petén region of modern day Guatemala.

Veracruz & Oaxaca

VERACRUZ & OAXACA
Classic Period, 200-900 CE

Classic Veracruz was closely connected to the cities of the Maya area, and both cultures shared many features from the earlier Olmec. Professional traders from Veracruz moved trade goods such as obsidian, jade, and pottery from central Mexico into the Maya area and became familiar with the cultures of both regions. The ancient cities of Veracruz, such as El Tajin, are filled with ball courts and the stone artwork that accompanied the game. In the stone carvings that decorate the largest ball court at El Tajin, ballplayers wearing stone yokes like the ones in this exhibition can be seen parading around the court. This important site is now an archaeological park and UNESCO World Heritage Center known for its impressive architecture.

West of Veracruz, the ancient cultures of Oaxaca clustered in high valleys and hilltop sites. The tripartite Valley of Oaxaca was occupied continuously from the Formative period through the Postclassic, and a series of terraces and irrigation systems allowed a large population to live in dense urban centers. Monte Alban is the best known archaeological site, where research throughout the 20th century recovered many carved monuments with a calendrical system of notations, astronomically aligned temples, and rich burial tombs. Elaborate art, such as the incense burners included in this exhibition, are characteristic of the type of gifts made for the important ancestors who lived in hundreds of underground chamber tombs. Deities familiar throughout ancient Mesoamerica, such as the Maize Deity and the Rain God, were often portrayed on these vessels. The dry environment of Oaxaca has left many of the ancient cities in an excellent state of conservation and their well preserved art and architecture make them striking places to visit even today.

Xipe Totec
Remojadas (Veracruz, Mexico)
ca. 450-650 CE
Ceramic
22 x 10 1/8 x 9 7/8"
Museum purchase through 35th Anniversary Funds, 86.0037

This magnificent ceramic sculpture of Xipe Totec, "our lord the flayed one", is one of the most beautiful and striking pieces in the Lowe Art Museum collection. The inherent visual impact of Xipe Totec figures has been skillfully recreated here using a combination of traditional iconography from Central Mexico with visual and technical elements of local Veracruz ceramic traditions. The incredibly naturalistic style is even more remarkable given the medium of clay; hollow ceramic sculpture of this quality is rare, especially in such an excellent state of conservation. This Xipe Totec priest is shown with the traditional human skin covering his body. The eyes are mostly closed and the mouth of the priest can be seen through an opening in the flayed skin. Hands and feet emerge from the "sleeves" of human skin. The impersonator wears large ear ornaments which are a common symbol of self-sacrifice in the ceramic sculpture of Veracruz. This type of Xipe Totec representation is a precursor of the much later Aztec versions in stone, one of which is included in this exhibition.

Sources: Goldstein (1987)

Ballgame Marker
Veracruz (Mexico)
ca. 600-900 CE
Stone
8 ½ x 5 ¼ x 6"
Museum purchase, 91.0038

Yokes, *palmas,* and *hachas,* are the three types of objects related to the ballgame found throughout Mesoamerica. Yokes may have been worn by ballplayers, while *palmas* and *hachas* were used to decorate the ball court. This *hacha* is similar in size to many others that have been found in Veracruz and is decorated with a human face in profile. The figure may be wearing a helmet given the deeply sunken eyes and zoomorphic nature of the nose and jaw. The ears are pierced, suggesting that ornaments may have been attached. The function of *hachas* is less certain than that of yokes, although they have most commonly been interpreted as markers for the ball game.

Ballgame Yoke
Veracruz (Mexico)
ca. 600-900 CE
Stone
4 ⅛ x 12 x 13 ¾"
Museum purchase, 90.0096

This yoke shows a high status individual emerging from the mouth of a reptile. The same motif repeats on the ends of the piece. Given the mythological associations of the ballgame and its linkage to the journey of the Hero Twins into the Underworld, reptiles and other animals associated with the earth in ancient Mesoamerica are frequently depicted on ballgame paraphernalia. These stone objects may have been templates for more practical yokes made of wood or leather but it is also possible that extremely skilled athletes could have worn such massive equipment on to a field of play.

Sources: *LAM* (1990, 2006), Matos (2003), Miller (2006)

Agricultural Deity or Priest Figure
Veracruz (Mexico)
ca. 1200-1400 CE
Stone
46"
Gift of Edward R. Roberts, 2006.31.11

This impressive stone sculpture from the Central Gulf Coast region represents an agricultural deity or a human priest wearing the ceremonial regalia for a harvest ritual. His face and body are depicted with incredible naturalism. The minimalistic ornamentation of the face and lower body allow the focus to remain on the elaborate headdress which is richly decorated with rosettes and serpents. A single open maw of a serpent is centered just above the face of the figure. His body language suggests movement and alertness. There is an obvious similarity to Aztec stone sculpture in dimension and style, but the fluidity of the figure reflects the translation of shared Postclassic ideas into the local figural style of Veracruz. Economically and politically the Aztec empire reached deep into the rich tributary Gulf lowlands but state art was not imposed upon the provinces. Local artistic production continued under the influence but not the control of the dominant state.

Sources: Miller (2006)

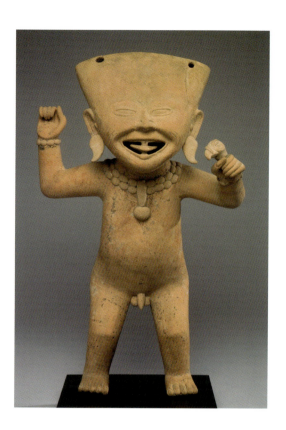

Figure
Veracruz (Mexico)
ca. 600–800 CE
Ceramic
22 x 13 1/8 x 5"
Gift of Edward R. Roberts, 2006.31.7

Smiling clay sculptures from the central Gulf of Mexico lowlands have become famous for their dynamic and lively expression. Each piece of this large standing object was made in an individual mold, then attached prior to firing. The Olmec were the first to use molds for figurine construction and the technique was still in use at the time of European contact. This figure has a triangular head with the typical "smiling" expression. He is naked except for a necklace, wristbands, and earrings. Holes at the top of his head would have allowed additional ornaments. Holding a rattle in one hand, like all the smiling figures, he seems ready to dance. The function of these lovely figures is debated, and some scholars suggest they represent musicians performing at ritual ceremonies, while others have interpreted the facial gesture as the painful grimace of a sacrificial victim. There may also be connections to monkeys, who were widely viewed as intelligent, playful and highly sexualized.

Sources: Goldstein (1987), Miller (2006), Taube (1988)

Funerary Urn
Zapotec (Oaxaca, Mexico)
ca. 600–800 CE
Ceramic
8 1/8 x 5 3/8 x 4"
Gift of Mr. and Mrs. Barry Fitzmorris, 2007.52.7

The bat is one of the most important animal deities of the Zapotec pantheon and this urn is also connected to Piquite Ziña, although in this example it is more likely we see a priest of the bat god wearing an elaborate costume. On this jar the bat is shown with an open mouth and projecting tongue, perhaps mimicking the way bats open their mouths during flight to echolocate. The ears are large and erect and he wears a chest pendant and a loincloth or *maxlatl*, two elements which serve to anthropomorphize the figure. The frontal position and the menacing gesture of palms and claws are also common conventions in the portrayal of the bat god. Throughout ancient Mesoamerica, the bat was linked to cave rituals and was seen as a deity related to the entrance of the Underworld. Its relevance is especially visible at the site of Monte Alban in modern Oaxaca, where numerous images of bats have been found in ceramic tomb offerings and carved in stone architecture. In the Popol Vuh, the Quiché Maya creation story, the House of Bats was one of the stages on the way to Xibalba, the underworld realm.

Sources: Caso (1952), Matos (2003), Sellen (2005)

Funerary Urn
Zapotec (Oaxaca, Mexico)
ca. 600-800 CE
Ceramic
6 5/8 x 5 x 3 1/2"
Gift of Dr. and Mrs. Allan A. Kaplan, 85.0072

The ceramic funerary urns found in Classic period Zapotec burials are some of the most distinctive artwork from ancient Mesoamerica. Often found in wall or floor niches in the most elaborate tombs, these anthropomorphic urns were re-used by ancient peoples and filled with perishable offerings when they were placed in a tomb. The bat god Piquite Ziña is depicted on this vessel. The loincloth and chest pendant, possibly a mirror, identify this deity. Red pigment has been applied to the mouth of the bat, the ear spools of the god and his mirror. The craftsperson that made this urn included anatomical details, such as incisors, that make it possible to identify this deity as a supernatural version of the leaf-nosed bat.

Sources: Kubler (1993), Marcus (1996), Sellen (2005)

Warrior Figure
Veracruz (Mexico)
ca. 200-400 CE
Ceramic
14 1/8 x 8 3/8 x 4"
Gift of Dr. and Mrs. Albert J. Kilberg, 94.0019.04

Warriors were a common subject of Gulf coast art. This figure wears an elaborate head dress and an intricate costume composed of a tunic, belted vest, bell necklace, and arm and ankle bands. His arms are raised and he seems ready to leap into action. The triangular shape of his head and facial features are reminiscent of traditional ceramic figures in the Remojadas style. The most striking feature of this piece is perhaps the figure's open mouth which seems about to speak a message of great importance. Images such as this warrior from Veracruz have been interpreted as representations of high status individuals and were included in residences, probably as part of ancestor worship rituals.

Sources: Townsend (2003)

Funerary Urn
Zapotec (Oaxaca, Mexico)
ca. 600-800 CE
Ceramic
6 x 6 1/8 x 4 1/2"
Gift of Dr. and Mrs. Allan A. Kaplan, 85.0073

Oaxacan funerary urns were made with a combination of mold made and hand made pieces, and in this example one can see how Zapotec potters experimented with the plasticity of the clay in order to create unique pieces. This miniature urn is a representation of a god with a serpent head dress. Large serpent profiles flank the deity and he wears a mask with a curling upper lip. The exaggerated earspools are typical of Zapotec iconography while the large chest pendant depicts a stylized flower motif.

Sources: Caso (1952), *LAM* (1990), Taube (1988), Sellen (2005)

Bowl
Veracruz (Mexico)
ca. 250-500 CE
Ceramic
4 ¼ x 7 ¼"
Gift of Roselillian Stoetzer, 2005.47.3

A plumed serpent and flower motifs decorate this polychrome ceramic bowl from Veracruz. The serpent circles the bowl and spots on the body of the serpent represent feathers. The rim is decorated with flower petals and a net motif can be seen in the background. This combination of snake and floral iconography is a recurring element in Mesoamerican art and may symbolize the eastern winds bringing precious rain.

Sources: Taube (2009)

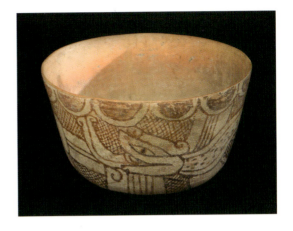

Central Mexico

CENTRAL MEXICO
Formative-Postclassic Periods, 200 BCE-1550 CE

The area west of the Isthmus of Tehuantepec was home to many varied and rich prehistoric cultures prior to the arrival of Hernán Cortez in 1519. Although tropical rainforest is found along the Gulf of Mexico coast farther north than Mexico City, much of Central Mexico is drier and higher in elevation than the rest of Mesoamerica. Pine forests and volcanic mountain ranges define the region and people occupied distinct valleys and basins. The modern megalopolis of Mexico City is situated atop the ancient Aztec capital of Tenochtitlan and adjacent to the earlier city of Teotihuacan. Today daily life is infused with remnants of the deep past for central Mexicans.

Teotihuacan was the first great city of ancient Mesoamerica, covered an area of more than 80 square kilometers, and may have had a population of a quarter of a million at its height in 400 CE. Hundreds of craft workshops fill the city and artists from throughout ancient Mesoamerica moved to Teotihuacan, bringing with them regional traditions and skills. Leaders were not portrayed in portraiture, nor was there a writing system to record dynastic history, so understanding how this massive city was governed is elusive. Stoic masks like those in this exhibit and the palace murals suggest an anonymous or unchanging aesthetic that remains both difficult and fascinating to modern eyes.

The Aztec Empire emerged from prophetic visions granted to one of the nomadic groups who lived north of the central Valley of Mexico in the early 13th century. They quickly founded their royal capital on an isolated island in the middle of Lake Texcoco and began campaigns of alliance and coercion within the region. By the time Cortez arrived only 200 years later, the Mexica had built an empire based on tribute payments and military conquest which extended throughout most of Central Mexico and down the Pacific coast to Guatemala. Professional traders who acted as spies for the royal dynasty moved goods and information back and forth throughout the region and maize agriculture was practiced in raised fields along well drained canals maintained by the state. Like earlier people of Mesoamerica, Aztec religion was filled with supernatural creatures who embodied the forces of nature, but the rain god Tlaloc and the tribal sun god Huitzilopochtli, were two of the most important deities.

Incense Burner Lid
Teotihuacan (Central Highlands, Mexico)
ca. 400-700 CE
Ceramic and mica
19 1/2 x 21 1/4 x 13 3/4"
Museum purchase, 89.0062

Elaborate ceramic incense burners or *incensarios* from Teotihuacan have been found as far south as Guatemala and Honduras, indicating the wide range of influence of this great Mesoamerican city. This lid is composed of a cylindrical core to which numerous ceramic and mica ornaments have been applied to create an intricate design. The central human figure wears a butterfly mask on the nose, a symbol associated with fertility and the spirits of the dead. The circular appliquéd pieces represent stone mirrors, artifacts widely used in Mesoamerica by shamans and priests for divination and other magical purposes. Incense burners were probably constructed and disassembled several times and served as dynamic portable shrines. Many have been found disassembled in burials and temple offerings. Ceramic production was a major economic activity in Teotihuacan and intense archaeological investigations in the area have revealed special sections of the city dedicated to the manufacture of these objects.

Sources: Berrin (1994), Evans (2008)

Tripod Bowl
Teotihuacan (Central Highlands, Mexico)
ca. 350-550 CE
Ceramic
10 1/8 x 12 1/8 x 12 1/2"
Gift of Roselillian Stoetzer, 2005.47.6

Elaborate tripod vessels such as this one are a trademark of Teotihuacan. This highly expressive tripod vessel is representative of the great skill Teotihuacan craft specialist developed in the first urban metropolis of ancient Mesoamerica. It has three images of a Monkey God with elaborate three dimensional faces applied to the vase. The body of the monkey is inscribed and he appears to be diving down to earth. This pose was commonly used to depict the way in which certain supernatural entities bestowed blessings, and it may have been modeled originally after the flight patterns of pollinating insects. The three slab feet are hollow, and each is also inscribed with similar images. Luxurious ceramic vessels from Teotihuacan, such as this have been found as offering in burials.

Sources: Berrin (1994)

Mask
Teotihuacan (Central Highlands, Mexico)
ca. 250-550 CE
Greenstone
8 1/4 x 8 3/4 x 4 5/8"
Gift of Edward R. Roberts, 2006.31.4

The masks made by artists at Teotihuacan are renowned for their impenetrable tranquility and are perhaps the most iconic art from this ancient city. Long the object of collectors, such masks have been found throughout Mesoamerica at sites like the Templo Mayor of Tenochtitlan, where they were appropriated by the Aztec elites as a symbol of prestige. The shape of classic Teotihuacan masks is standardized, with the basic features formed by intersecting horizontal and vertical planes carved in stone. This mask, made of precious greenstone, has eyes and teeth which were originally inlayed with shell, obsidian, or pyrite. It shows the typical wide forehead, robust nose, and linear eyes and mouth. The rectangular ears are pierced, indicating that ornaments of jade or metal were probably attached. Despite the basic standardization in the general shape of these masks, with predominately square or rectangular configurations, there is great variation in detail and visual expression in each individual piece. This mask achieves the greatest naturalistic effect of the three included in this exhibit.

Mask
Teotihuacan (Central Highlands, Mexico)
ca. 250-550 CE
Greenstone
8 1/2 x 8 1/2 x 5 1/8"
Gift of Mr. and Mrs. Barry Fitzmorris, 2007.52.2

A square shape contrasts sharply with the prominently triangular nose of this human face. The eyes and eyebrows have been reduced to simple horizontal lines. The natural pattern of the greenstone provides the mask with a lively effect despite the minimalistic rendering of its facial features. The specific function of Teotihuacan masks is uncertain but they have been interpreted as elements of funerary bundles. The holes in the ears, and occasionally in the forehead, indicate that they may have been attached to larger objects such as an effigy made of perishable materials.

Source: Berrin (1994)

Incense Burner
Teotihuacan (Central Highlands, Mexico)
ca. 350-550 CE
Ceramic and iron pyrite
20 x 15 3/4 x 9 1/4"
Gift of Mr. and Mrs. Robert Stoetzer, 91.0367

This more modest incense burner has less decorative elements than others but the same "theatre" shape and basic attributes, such as the naturalistic depiction of a human figure wearing a butterfly nose mask. In this piece we see how the ornate lid is matched with a lower receptacle for burning resin incense. Throughout Mesoamerica incense burners were decorated with the spikes of a young ceiba (*Ceiba pentandra*) tree, visible here. Three mirrors adorn the top band with a prominent floral symbol below the face. The butterfly mask motif has been replicated at the base.

Sources: Berrin (1994)

Female Figure Nursing an Infant
Teotihuacan (Central Highlands, Mexico)
ca. 350-550 CE
Ceramic
7 7/8 x 5 x 3 5/8"
Gift of David M. Stoetzer, 2005.51.4

Similar to the traditions of Colima and Nayarit, ceramic figurines from Teotihuacan depict the daily activities of its citizens, and allow us to explore the cultural practices of these ancient populations. This figure of a seated woman holding her infant child demonstrates the great importance placed upon motherhood by ancient Mesoamericans. Given her large earspools, green stone necklace, and elaborate hair style we know she is a high status individual. The beautiful naturalistic style of this piece, with great attention to the braid of hair hanging down this figure's back as well as the tiny hand of the baby conveys a dignity that was the ideal of femininity in ancient Teotihuacan. Most ceramic figurines found at Teotihuacan were located in household contexts suggesting that they were closely related to daily domestic rituals.

Sources: Berrin (1994)

Mask
Teotihuacan (Central Highlands, Mexico)
ca. 250-550 CE
Serpentine, shell and obsidian
8 1/2 x 7 5/8 x 5 1/4"
Gift of Mr. and Mrs. Barry Fitzmorris, 2008.30.1

This mask retains stone and shell inlays that accentuate the eyes and teeth. Large black pupils made of the volcanic stone obsidian animate this mask in a very different way than the other examples in this exhibit. The oval form of the face and arched eyebrows lend a gentler overall appearance but the strong nose remains a prominent feature as in all the Teotihuacan masks. The great ritual power of these objects is exemplified with this piece, which vividly preserves a living and expressive appearance.

Chicomecoatl, The Maize Goddess
Aztec (Central Valley, Mexico)
ca. 1350-1550 CE
Basalt
19 5/8 x 7 5/8 x 6 3/8"
Museum purchase, 56.003.000

This stone sculpture represents Chicomecoatl, the Aztec goddess of maize. Her name means "seven serpent" in Nahuatl, a reference to the day when her festival was celebrated. Within the complex maize iconography of ancient Mesoamerica, images of Chicomecoatl symbolize the ripe maize plant and the general concept of sustenance. The Chicomecoatl in the collection of the Lowe is a beautiful example of Aztec sculptural values. The figure is perfectly symmetrical with a calm or even static expression. In this piece we can see the face of the goddess impersonator emerge from the elaborate headdress while she holds two maize ears or rattles in her hands. Her dress is very simple with only a rope that ties at her waist. The figure's hands and feet are disproportionately large and carved with greater detail than the rest of the body, a common feature of Chicomecoatl representations which were often covered in the red pigment associated with the goddess. The highly standardized form and abundance of Chicomecoatl images suggests that they were mass-produced in Aztec times and possibly used in household rituals.

Sources: Baquedano (1984), Miller (2006), Sahagún (1992), Townsend (2000)

Pendant
Mexico
ca. 200-1550 CE
Rock crystal
3 1/4 x 2 x 7/8"
Gift of Enrico Varisco in memory of Roberto Varisco, 2003.63.3

Rock crystal was used in Aztec art primarily for smaller-scale ornaments and body decoration. Thought difficult to carve, the transparency of this material made it highly desirable for sculptors, whose excellent craftsmanship can be seen in the careful carving of the eyes, angular eyebrows, nose, and semi-opened mouth. The hair, or perhaps helmet, is formed by intersecting grooves which create a net. Small human heads or masks such as this one were worn as chest pendants throughout Mesoamerica from Olmec times until the arrival of Europeans and had significant ritual connotations.

Sources: *LAM* (2003)

Dog
Mexico
ca. 200-1550 CE
Stone
1 x 7/8 x 1 3/4"
Gift of Enrico Varisco in memory of Roberto Varisco, 2003.63.6

One of the few domesticated animals in ancient Mesoamerica was the dog. Dogs were significant in both ritual and daily life, and they were widely represented in ceramic, stone and more perishable carvings. The Aztecs saw these animals as essential companions in the voyage to the Underworld after death, as they were responsible for guiding humans through the numerous tasks to be completed before arriving in Mictlan, the land of the dead. Despite its miniature dimensions, this image of a dog is a remarkable example of Aztec stone sculpture. The figure is well proportioned with cheerful eyes and open mouth. A long curling tail rests on its back. The color and polished surface of the stone emphasize the symbolic importance of the animal.

Sources: Baquedano (1984), Evans (2008), Matos (1988)

Coyote Head
Aztec (Central Valley, Mexico)
ca. 1350-1550 CE
Rock crystal
2 1/2 x 2 x 4 5/8"
77.324.001

Coyotes were powerful predators and the patrons of elite warrior orders. This coyote head is skillfully carved in rock crystal, a difficult mineral to work. The snout, eyes and mouth are elegantly formed, and the ears are represented by a graceful spiral, a feature that appears commonly in Aztec animal sculpture. Several holes in the back suggest that it was originally attached to a staff or costume.

Sources: *LAM* (2003), Pasztory (1983)

Anthropomorphic Turtle
Aztec (Central Valley, Mexico)
ca. 1350-1550 CE
Basalt
8 1/2 x 17 1/4 x 14 1/2"
Gift of The Rubin-Ladd Foundation, 2009.41.8

This piece is a magnificent example of Aztec sculptural skill and interest in animal representations. This turtle image is carved on all sides, typical of the Aztec sculptural tradition. The carapace shows well-defined scutes, and underneath a human figure emerges showing only the head, hands and feet. This figure is likely Ehecatl, the Aztec god of wind, who wears a mask, tubular nose ornament and a pair of large ear spools. Stone images of real or mythological animals with anthropomorphic body parts are common in Mesoamerican art. This hybridization is closely related to an aspect of the Mesoamerican worldview, which allowed the translation of dualities observed in nature (animal/human, earthly/divine) into highly symbolic art forms. Turtles were important in Aztec mythology and were associated with water, earth, and fertility. Several examples of turtle representations in stone and ceramic, along with the remains of actual specimens, have been found as part of offerings in archaeological sites throughout Mexico City.

Sources: Alcina (1992); Carrasco (2003); Pasztory (1983)

Miniature Grinding Stone
Mexico
ca. 1000-1550
Basalt
1 1/8 x 5 1/2 x 3 5/8"
Gift of Dr. and Mrs. Albert J. Kilberg, 94.0019.14

Grinding stones are ubiquitous artifacts in Mesoamerica. They were used to grind corn to produce masa and tortillas, and for many other purposes. Essentially unchanged for almost 8000 years, these objects are important indicators of economy, social structure, and gender relations when found on archaeological sites. This miniature grinding stone has a simple rectangular shape carved from a flat basalt stone slab with ridges around the borders. Given its small size it was likely used to grind pigments or other precious minerals to make paint and cosmetics.

Source: Evans (2008)

Spindle Whorls
Aztec (Central Valley, Mexico)
ca. 1350-1550 CE
Ceramic
7/8 x 2", 5/8 x 1 7/8"
Gift of C. Clay Aldridge, S2003.51.114 & S2003.51.115

Ceramic spindle whorls were used for spinning cotton and maguey fibers into thread. The thickness of the thread depended on the size and weight of the whorl: for thinner cotton thread, smaller whorls were used with a small vessel to balance the spindle. These two examples are profusely decorated with floral and geometric motifs which derive from the close association between spinning and Xochiquetzal, the Aztec goddess of flowers who is also closely associated with birds. Because we know that spinning and weaving were closely associated with ideals of female identity in Aztec times, spindle whorls are especially relevant when interpreting gender identity and household economy in archaeological contexts.

Source: Blumfiel (1996)

Labret
Aztec (Central Valley, Mexico)
ca. 1350–1550
Obsidian
3/8 x 1 x 3/8"
Gift of Enrico Varisco in memory of Roberto Varisco, 2003.63.24

Ornaments such as this obsidian labret or lip plug were worn as status markers by Aztec elites and played a key role in rites of passage. Thin obsidian ear spools, labrets, and lip pendants indicated the wearer's position, wealth, and even age. This perfectly preserved labret is typical of many that have been found in burials and caches.

Sources: Matos (2003)

Bowl
Aztec (Central Valley, Mexico)
ca. 1350–1550
Basalt and specular hematite
10 x 10 5/8 x 9 1/8"
Gift of Drs. Ann and Robert Walzer, 2008.38.12

The god of rain and thunder was a ubiquitous figure in ancient Mesoamerica from the earliest settlements to European contact. In Central Mexico he was known as Tlaloc, first at Teotihuacan and then much later at the Aztec capital of Tenochtitlan, where he shared the main temple structure with the war god Huitzilopochtli. Many vessels decorated with Tlaloc have been found since his association with rain and water made liquid a particularly suitable offering to the god.

This Tlaloc vessel is made of volcanic stone, a material often utilized for ritual offerings. On it we can see the traditional visual attributes of the god: goggle eyes, nose and eyebrows formed by a twisted serpent, and prominent fangs springing from the mouth. The colors associated with Tlaloc, red and blue, are very vividly preserved on this piece. It has a globular shape with small handles on both sides. Several of the most beautiful and sophisticated Tlaloc vessels have been found in dedication offerings at the Templo Mayor.

Source: Matos (1988); (2003)

Vase
Mexico (Central Valley)
ca. 300-1550
Onyx
8 x 9 3/4 x 6"
Gift of Enrico Varisco in memory of Roberto Varisco, 2003.63.69

This three legged onyx vase is made from a single solid block of lustrous white and black banded onyx. Two animal heads, possibly jaguars or another large feline, have been carved as handles. Mexican onyx has been mined since antiquity in the state of Puebla. The Aztecs called this material *tecali*, or "house of stone." The texture, colors and contour of the stone have been utilized skillfully as the only decoration, turning a traditionally utilitarian form into a delicate luxury piece.

Source: Matos (1988)

Male Figure
Aztec (Central Valley, Mexico)
ca. 1350-1550 CE
Basalt
10 3/8 x 3 3/4 x 3 1/8"
Gift of Mr. and Mrs. Barry Fitzmorris, 2007.52.15

Macehualli are standardized sculptural representations of male figures found as part of Aztec offerings, particularly at the Templo Mayor in Tenochtitlan. They represent the ideal common man. This example has the typical rigid posture and stern expression, but also well-defined facial features and a particularly lively expression, emphasized by the unusual position of the hands crossed over the chest. The excellent carving skill of Aztec artists is evident, especially in the eyes, nose, and mouth, and in the detailed execution of the sandals and feet. Curiously this piece lacks the typical orifice in the chest area, which might have contained inlays of jade, gold, or other precious stones to indicate the heart, a feature present in most examples of this sculptural type.

Sources: Baquedano (1984), Matos (2003), Nicholson (1983)

Tripod Bowl
Guerrero (Pacific Coast, Mexico)
ca. 900-1500 CE
Ceramic
5 1/2 x 11 1/2 x 11 3/8"
Gift of May Cassard, 86.0213

The Mixteca-Puebla style of the post-Classic period originated in Central Mexico and was transported throughout much of Mesoamerica, where local ceramic traditions produced beautiful pieces such as this one. This bowl has the common tripod shape and is adorned with geometric and symbolic motifs associated with earth and sky. The brightness of the red and white pigment decoration exemplifies the excellent firing technique of Pacific coast potters. Finished polychrome vessels like this one were traded widely throughout Mesoamerica.

Sources: *LAM* (1990), Kubler (1990)

Tripod Bowl
Mixtec (Valley of Oaxaca, Central Mexico); Aztec (Central Valley, Mexico)
ca. 1200-1550 CE
Ceramic
5 7/8 x 9 1/4 x 10"
Gift of Enrico Varisco in memory of Roberto Varisco, 2003.63.10

Mixtec artists from the Valley of Oaxaca in southern Mexico were highly accomplished craftspeople well before the Aztecs made political incursions into their homeland. Eventually a large population of Mixtec potters lived in the Aztec capital of Tenochtitlan. This tripod bowl is completely covered with geometric and water motifs. The designs are beautifully executed in vibrant red, white, and black. The interior rim is adorned with volutes which suggest the movement of water. The bright colors and the fine delineation of this bowl's motifs exemplify the excellent polychrome technique achieved by Mixtec potters and many similar vessels have been found in burials and temple dedications in the Aztec capital of Tenochtitlan.

Sources: Miller (2006)

Xipe Totec
Aztec (Central Valley, Mexico)
ca. 1350-1550
Basalt
11 1/2 x 6 x 8"
Gift of The Rubin - Ladd Foundation, 2008.39.20

The god Xipe Totec "our lord the flayed one," symbolized the regeneration of the earth's vegetation each spring and the harvest of corn each fall. Xipe Totec priests would wear the skin of a sacrificial victim for twenty days or until it fell rotten from their bodies to symbolize the ability of life to spring from death. The images of Xipe Totec, like the one in the Lowe collection, are easily recognizable by the flayed skin worn by a priest. The skin is tied at the back of the body and the eyes and mouth of the wearer emerge from facial openings. The great number of Xipe Totec images found throughout Mesoamerica reveals the widespread practice of his rituals as one of the most significant deities of agriculture and fertility. His representations are usually striking to the Western viewer given the apparent contrast between the calm attitude of the priest and the intrinsic violence of the ritual.

Sources Miller (2006), Nicholson (1983)

Squash
Aztec (Central Valley, Mexico)
ca. 1350-1550 CE
Basalt
12 1/8 x 5 1/8 x 4 1/2"
Gift of The Rubin - Ladd Foundation, 2008.39.14

Aztecs artists often chose to portray culturally important plants and animals in a careful and naturalistic style. This carving depicts with great detail the irregularities of the fruit, and the final product has been carefully polished, creating an extremely realistic image. Though squash sculptures such as this one have no clear provenience, it has been suggested that they were part of offerings, possibly associated with agricultural rituals. But the great visual quality of these pieces, usually represented with breathtaking realism, has also led some to suggest that they were meant to be on display in temples dedicated to fertility.

Sources: Alcina (1992), Nicholson (1983)

Feathered Coyote
Aztec (Central Valley, Mexico)
ca. 1350-1550
Basalt
11 1/2 x 6 x 8"
Gift of The Rubin - Ladd Foundation, 2008.39.23

Throughout North and Central America, the coyote is seen as a trickster and a rich oral tradition has developed around this creature. Aztec artists excelled at the naturalistic depiction of mythological themes and this piece may represent the *xiuhcoyotl* or "turquoise coyote," a powerful mascot of one of the Aztec warrior societies. Several stone feathered coyotes have been found, but this example from the Lowe is one of the more gentle examples. The artist paid careful attention to the limbs, paws, and facial features, and chose to portray the feathers at rest which gives this coyote a pleasant and well behaved appearance.

Sources: *LAM* (2003), Carrasco (2003)

Pendant
Mezcala (Central Mexico)
ca. 300 BCE-300 CE
Greenstone
1 1/2 x 2 1/8 x 3/8"
Gift of The Institute of Maya Studies, 80.0061

Stone pendants from the Mezcala river region, in the modern state of Guerrero, are much less common than the iconic temple models found in Aztec offerings. The beauty of the stonework is what makes this piece important. The simplicity of shape coupled with the expertly polished surface turned abundant river stone into portable luxury objects. Given the highly abstract nature of Mexcala art, this pendant may represent a radically schematized human face.

Sources: Evans (2008), Miller (2006), Taube (1988)

Temple Model
Mezcala (Central Mexico)
ca. 300 BCE-300 CE
Stone
3 1/4 x 2 5/8 x 1 1/8"
Gift of The Rubin - Ladd Foundation, 2007.4.16

Temple models from the Mezcala river region in modern Guerrero are remarkable for their simplicity and beautiful craftsmanship. This temple model shows an architectural structure with two massive columns supporting a rectangular roof. The building is set upon a platform which is surmounted via a narrow set of stairs. The smooth surface of the stone, which was carved using a thread-saw technique, helps accentuate the elegant lines of this quasi-abstract composition.

Guerrero is famous for these temple models which the Aztec demanded their conquered subjects in Guerrero pay in tribute. A handful of provenienced examples suggest these objects may have been used in dedication rituals for new buildings. The pure lines and strong schematic character of these pieces make them one of the most original sculptural types in Mesoamerica.

Sources: Evans (2008), Miller (2006)

Temple Model
Mezcala (Central Mexico)
ca. 300 BCE- 300 CE
Stone
7 1/2 x 4 5/8 x 3/4"
Gift of The Rubin - Ladd Foundation, 2007.4.17

This Mezcala style temple model shows four columns on top of a platform with a narrow stairway. A small anthropomorphic figure stands on the roof. This enigmatic feature is seen in other temple models from the Mezcala river region and it may represent the owner or spirit of the temple. The model has been cut from a quadrangular stone piece, and the color and brightness of the stone have been enhanced by the skillful polishing technique. Temple models from Guerrero lack any resemblance to local architectural styles, and instead show significant influences from important sites such as Monte Alban in Oaxaca.

Sources: Evans (2008), Miller (2006)

Figure
Mezcala (Central Mexico)
ca. 300 BCE- 300 CE
Greenstone
5 1/2 x 2 1/8 x 1 3/8"
Gift of Mr. and Mrs. Barry Fitzmorris, 2006.36.5

This human figure illustrates the schematic characteristics typical of the Mezcala Style. The head is oval with barely delineated facial features. Both arms and legs have been cut into the rock in a deliberately simple way. Hundreds of human figurines such as this one, made from highly prized green stone, were found in the different construction stages of the Templo Mayor in the Aztec capital of Tenochtitlan. Their careful positioning facing south, and their distribution on several stone offering boxes have led scholars to suggest such figures illustrate the significance of the rich Guerrero region for the economic and political success of the Aztecs.

Sources: Matos (2003), Reyna (2003)

West Mexico

WEST MEXICO
Formative Period, 300 BCE-300 CE

Some of the most common and beloved objects in museum collections are large hollow ceramic figurines from western Mexico, especially the modern states of Jalisco, Nayarit, and Colima. For many years these figurines were the only information available about the ancient cultures of this region, an area of high desert near the foothills of the Sierra Madre Occidental mountain range where agriculture prior to modern irrigation was difficult. Briefly brought under the control of the Aztec Empire, for much of their history the tribes of western Mexico lived independently and traded sporadically with other cultures. They shared the same economic basis in maize agriculture, and appear to have played the ball game, but in many other ways their cultural practices reflected their location on the northern frontier of Mesoamerica.

West Mexican ceramic figurines were made as funerary offerings and placed in burials known as shaft tombs. Large chambers dug into the underlying volcanic tuff, often by means of a single shaft 3-20 meters long, were used as family mausoleums and held the remains of many people. Only certain families had the power to organize the labor required to construct such a tomb and commission the artwork included in them. Pairs of large male and female figures like those in this exhibition were a common offering and may represent lineage founders or important ancestors. The famous pot bellied dogs were also common offerings, and while they may represent dogs raised for food, they may also represent companions on the journey after death. Like much of the art of ancient Mesoamerica, humans with unusual features or supernatural characteristics related to the practice of shamanism were also important offerings to the dead.

Shaman Figure
Colima (Pacific Coast, Mexico)
ca. 300 BCE–300 CE
Ceramic
14 x 9 1/8 x 5 1/4"
Museum purchase through 35th Anniversary Funds, 85.0010

This shaman or warrior figure is one of the most expressive objects from the west Mexican collection at the Lowe. His raised right arm holds an axe in a menacing gesture. In his other hand is a trophy head. A second figure emerges from the shaman's torso with its head between his legs. While reminiscent of human birth the main figure is clearly male following the gendered conventions of Colima art. Perhaps the shaman is giving birth to another shaman such as his apprentice or spirit helper. However the second body, whose limbs, head, and torso are clearly visible, could also be a representation of the skin of a dead captive or sacrificial victim in keeping with the trophy head held in the shaman's left hand. The horn on his forehead may be a symbol of his status, and similar figures have also been interpreted as warriors. Despite the emotionless expression, the posture and visual attributes are powerful enough to transmit a sense of vitality and awe.

Sources: *LAM* (1990), Reynolds (1993)

Helmeted Male Figure
Nayarit (Pacific Coast, Mexico)
ca. 300 BCE-300 CE
Ceramic
27 x 9 1/8 x 6 3/4"
Gift of Mr. and Mrs. Samuel J. Levin, 62.044.003

Female Figure with Dog
Nayarit (Pacific Coast, Mexico)
ca. 300 BCE-300 CE
Ceramic
23 1/2 x 10 x 5 1/2"
Gift of Mr. and Mrs. Samuel J. Levin, 62.044.005

These figures are powerful examples of the Nayarit ceramic figurine tradition. Covered in red slip paint, they include the characteristic clothing styles and ornaments that identify effigies from this region. Both figures wear multiple ear and nose rings for decoration and lines around the face indicate tattoos or scarification. The male figure is dressed in a shirt tied at one shoulder and a modest loincloth. His pointed hat shows a zigzag pattern in white over red. The female figure wears a simple wrap skirt of decorated cloth and other elaborate jewelry. All the garments are profusely decorated with abstract geometric designs in black and white over red slip paint. These characters are among the most expressive figures in Mesoamerican ceramic art.

Sources: Kan (1970), *LAM* (1990)

Female Figurine
Nayarit (Pacific Coast)
ca. 300 BCE-300 CE
Ceramic
16 3/8 x 7 x 3 1/2
Gift of May Cassard, 86.0212

Traces of the original orange-red slip and black paint remain on this female ceramic figurine from Nayarit. The image shows no decorative elements, an unusual trait for figural art from western Mexico. A lack of decoration highlights the curvilinear female body with voluptuous hips and thighs. Both hands encircle the breasts and rest delicately over the abdomen. The heart-shaped head, coffee-bean eyes and overall simplicity correspond to the so called "Chinesco" sub-style from Nayarit. Usually found in shaft tomb contexts, Nayarit ceramic figurines traditionally have been interpreted as burial offerings.

Source: Kan (1970)

Temple Model
Nayarit (Pacific Coast, Mexico)
ca. 300 BCE-300 CE
Ceramic
10 x 5 1/2 x 8 3/4"
Museum purchase, 91.0010

Nayarit art commonly depicts group scenes in architectural settings. While many of these are peaceful domestic events or communal celebrations such as the ballgame, this temple model has a more explicitly ritual focus. Elevated on a large supporting platform, this temple has a pyramidal roof and steep staircase. A human figure, clearly a sacrificial victim, lays motionless on the stairs with a deep chest wound, an indication that a sacrifice has been performed and the victim's heart has been removed as an offering to the gods. This temple model offers a powerful representation of one of the most extensive of Mesoamerican religious practices. Sacrifice was seen as necessary for the origin and maintenance of the cosmos and human life, and was a complex and thoughtful process. The Nayarit tradition is characterized by a great variety of themes depicted in three dimensional ceramic objects, and the dramatic representation of ritual sacrifice seen in this piece serves as a vivid reminder of the central role religion played in the lives of ancient Mesoamerican people.

Figure Tied to Slab
Colima (Pacific Coast, Mexico)
ca. 300 BCE-300 CE
Ceramic
3 x 1 5/8 x 3/4"
Gift of Dr. and Mrs. Allan A. Kaplan, 80.0115

This simple figure represents a war captive or sacrificial victim. The figure is tied to a large rock and even the highly abstracted facial features convey despair and pain. The long nose, elongated forehead and coffee-bean eyes, resemble the "Gingerbread" sub-style within the Colima ceramic tradition. The depiction of a captive is rare in Colima ceramic figurines which generally emphasize everyday life.

Sources: Reynolds (1993)

Jar
Colima (Pacific Coast, Mexico)
ca. 300 BCE-300 CE
Ceramic
9 3/8 x 13 1/4"
Gift of Edward R. Roberts, 2006.31.14

The extraordinary technical skills of Colima ceramic artists are visible in this piece despite its simple form. The upper surface of the pot is decorated with the calendric glyph, "5 reed," which marks the celebration of Chalchiuhtlicue, the Aztec goddess of ground water. Iconography related to water deities was a common decoration. The design was carved after the firing process which is characteristic of Colima ceramic production. Just like the rest of the human and animal figures from Colima included in this exhibit, this jar was likely placed in a shaft tomb as a mortuary offering.

Sources: Boone (2007), Kan (1970)

Female Figure
Jalisco (Pacific Coast, Mexico)
ca. 300 BCE-300 CE
Ceramic
9 3/4 x 5 7/8 x 7 1/2"
Gift of Marlene and Marvin Padover, 94.0021.06

Figurines from Jalisco in the "Ameca Gray" style such as this one are characterized by remarkable cranial elongation. This female figure sits in a casual pose with her arm resting upon a raised knee. Her other arm surrounds one of her breasts, which are well defined with appliqué nipples. The long nose and large staring eyes are also characteristic of the Ameca style. Jalisco figurines have recurring themes, and this piece exemplifies the "thinker" figures, which are usually female with asymmetrical leg positions and serene facial expressions. Most female representations in Mesoamerican art show women engaged in traditional female activities such as childcare or food preparation. However, a large number of female figurines from Jalisco are depicted in actions that depart from this traditionally gendered focus.

Sources: Kan (1970), *LAM* (1990)

Figure with Bowl
Jalisco (Pacific Coast, Mexico)
ca. 300 BCE-300 CE
Ceramic
10 1/8 x 6 1/2 x 4 3/4"
Gift from the Collection of Edward and Louise Lipton, 2002.18.32

This figurine belongs to the "pot-maker" group of Jalisco hollow figurines. He has the typical elongated cranium covered by elaborate head gear with crossing bands. His face shows the characteristic long nose and ears, and slit-like minimalistic eyes. The figure is sitting and holds an unfinished pot between his legs, suggesting that he might be in the process of working on the vessel. The red and white bands of the pot show the level of detail this artist intended to convey, as well as the magnificent modeling and firing skills achieved by Jalisco ceramicists. This figure represents not only a beautiful example of the Jalisco style, but it also offers an intimate look into an economic activity of significant importance to ancient Mesoamerican peoples.

Sources: Kan (1970)

Female Dwarf Holding a Staff
Colima (Pacific Coast, Mexico)
ca. 300 BCE-300 CE
Ceramic
12 3/8 x 8 5/8 x 6 1/2"
Gift of Julien Balogh, 76.035.002

In west Mexican cultures dwarfs were believed to have shamanic powers. This female dwarf figure is an excellent example of the Colima figural ceramic tradition that portrayed the human condition in great detail. She has a prominent nose and lips, but her eyes lack expression. Her ears are pierced with noticeable holes for additional ornaments. Her breasts are barely suggested, and she lacks her left hand. A simple red skirt is the only clothing depicted and is typical of women in Colima figurines.

Sources: *LAM* (1990), Reynolds (1993)

Hunchback Figure
Colima (Pacific Coast, Mexico)
ca. 300 BCE-300 CE
Ceramic
11 x 10 1/4 x 10 3/4"
Museum purchase through 35th Anniversary Funds, 86.0208

Elegance and exquisite manufacture are qualities that make Colima ceramic vessels attractive to the modern eye. The beautiful finish of this crouching hunchback figure makes it a remarkable example of the Colima tradition. Red slip paint was applied when the piece had air dried, then it was carefully burnished for hours with a soft stone before finally being fired. The deformed body of the figure is marked by a prominent hump on the back and a blade-like deformation of both tibia bones. He has a long nose, thin lips and eyes, and pierced ear lobes. His head is covered by a tightly fitting skull cap. The abdominal muscles, umbilicus, and sexual organs are also depicted. In west Mexican tradition, hunchbacks were believed to have magical or shamanic powers. They lived apart from the rest of society and were cared for by attendants.

Sources: Kan (1970), *LAM* (1990)

Armadillo Effigy Vessel
Colima (Pacific Coast, Mexico)
ca. 300 BCE-300 CE
Ceramic
6 1/2 x 14 3/8 x 6"
Museum purchase, 89.0160

Animal effigy vessels are a very common theme in west Mexican ceramic art. Dogs are the most common subject but other animals were also depicted such as this armadillo. The head, neck, and legs emerge from the large carapace that covers the animal's body and the tail serves as the vessel's spout. The type of abstraction that was mastered by Central Mexican sculptors has led some scholars to interpret similar pieces as representations of small dogs dressed in turtle shells.

Sources: *LAM* (1990), Reynolds (1993)

Clown Figure or Phallic Dancer
Colima (Pacific Coast, Mexico)
ca. 300 BCE-300 CE
Ceramic
21 1/8 x 9 1/2 x 6 3/4"
Museum purchase, 89.0026

Male figurines from Colima with exaggerated sexual organs have generally been labeled "Phallic Dancers". While the actual meaning of these figures remains obscure given how rarely they have been discovered in archaeological context, the strong visual emphasis on the erect phallus points to ritual connotations associated with fertility and inversion. Clowns were important on many ritual occasions in ancient Mesoamerica and often reinforced cultural norms through ridicule. This figure portrays a priest or a shaman wearing a ritual costume. His face is covered by a mask with enormous rounded eyes, pointed nose, and menacing teeth. A miniature ceramic vessel forms the spout on top of his head. The figure wears a tight shirt or vest and a girdle with the large phallus attached. On each leg he has a pair of disc-shaped ornaments. As in most Colima human representations, the hands and feet are absent and the limbs have been reduced to their basic conceptual form.

Sources: Kan (1970), *LAM* (1990)

Costa Rica & Panama

COSTA RICA & PANAMA
Formative-Postclassic Periods, 200 BCE-1550 CE

At the crossroads of north and south, the ancient cultures of Costa Rica and Panama developed their own unique expression of Mesoamerican beliefs and practices. Drawing upon a rich tropical environment punctuated with coastal inlets, the people of this region were organized into villages of up to 1000 inhabitants and lived under the protection of a chief. Comparatively less investigation has been done of the ancient settlements of Costa Rica and Panama, although visitors can enjoy sites such as Guayabo National Monument in the Cartago province of Costa Rica, in addition to the well known rainforests and beaches of this region.

There are three main ancient cultures in Costa Rica and Panama and while unique, all were in regular contact with one another and the other peoples of Mesoamerica. To the north and west is Greater Nicoya, located in the Nicoya Peninsula, Guanacaste province, and southern Nicaragua. It was most closely tied to the cultures of the north such as the Maya and Aztec, and by 500 CE chiefdoms in this area engaged in long distance trade with their neighbors for luxury items. Jade from Costa Rica has been found at Olmec sites and Maya style jade ornaments have been found in Costa Rica. Whether artists were moving back and forth or only the raw material has yet to be determined. After 800, Greater Nicoya was settled by people who spoke central Mexican languages and brought their local artistic and ball game traditions with them.

The central part of Costa Rica, from the Atlantic coastal plains through the interior uplands is known as the Central Highlands. This is where competing chiefdoms perfected stone carving techniques, using the plentiful volcanic stone in the region. Corn grinding stones and low thrones are both common artifacts, and each were elaborately decorated with important animals such as the jaguar. Leaders would occasionally preserve the heads of captives caught in battle but trophy heads were also made from stone, as we can see in this exhibition.

On the southeastern frontier of Costa Rica and the northern provinces of Panama is a culture known as Greater Chiriquí which was closely tied to the ancient cultures of Colombia. Gold and other metal-working traditions spread north from South America and were perfected by the ancient artists of this region into iconic personal ornaments of animals and supernatural creatures. Gold symbolized the power of the sun, and replaced jade in this area as the highest status adornment around the year 800.

Jar
Greater Nicoya (Costa Rica)
ca. 1000-1350 CE
Ceramic
15 x 10 1/2 x 12 3/4"
Gift of Seymour Rosenberg, 72.016.009

The polychrome ceramics of Costa Rica have long been admired for their fine manufacture and brilliant colors. Even in antiquity they were widely traded north into the rest of Mesoamerica where they influenced local ceramic traditions. This large Pataky Polychrome jar is a fine example of later Costa Rican polychrome art. A crouching jaguar has been added to the pear shaped vessel, and the modeled jaguar head includes an open mouth with snarling teeth. Geometric bands in orange and gray along the rim and foot of the vessel symbolize the upper and lower worlds, positioning the jaguar as the master of the surface of the earth. Pataky is characterized by a large ovoid or pear shape body on a pedestal support, while the colors used were most often orange, red, and black on a white or cream slip. The jaguar iconography is representative of a man/jaguar myth, which was quite common among late period ceramics and is a defining feature of this style.

Sources: Day (1982), Snarskis and Blanco (1978)

Male Figure with Trophy Head
Central Highlands/Atlantic Watershed (Costa Rica)
Ca.1000-1550 CE
Basalt
22 ³/₈ x 10 ¹/₈ x 6 ³/₈"
Gift of Alfred I. Barton, 62.045.003

Large, freestanding, stone sculptures of warriors returning from battle were common in the Atlantic Watershed Region during the last centuries before European contact. Increased population pressure made warriors an important part of the success of each chiefdom. This male warrior figure holds an ax in one hand and has a trophy head suspended over his shoulder. Carved from a single block of basalt, this figure may have been displayed prior to burial with an important ancestor. Warriors brought trophy heads back from battle as proof of their success and to enhance their status in the community.

Source: Esquivel (2006)

Whistle
Central Highlands/Atlantic Watershed (Costa Rica)
ca. 500-1000 CE
Ceramic
2 ¹/₄ x 4 ⁷/₈ x 1 ³/₈"
Museum purchase, 65.050.058

The collared peccary *(Tayassu tajacu)* is a large mammal native to the American tropics and one of the preferred game animals of indigenous populations. Social creatures that live in herds, they are not threatening to humans unless provoked. This simple whistle celebrates the jovial nature of peccaries, and suggests that these creatures were celebrated in rituals or feasts. The double-headed design of this piece may be due to the social habits of this animal or may be a stylistic feature as seen on the jaguar ocarina also included in this exhibition.

Rattle
Central Highlands/Atlantic Watershed (Costa Rica)
ca. 1-800 CE
Ceramic
3 1/4 h. x 1 1/4"
Museum purchase, 85.0004

Music and song were remarkably important in the ritual and daily lives of ancient Mesoamericans. From painted vessels we know small musical instruments like rattles and gourds were used in nearly all ceremonies, and their ubiquitous presence suggests that such items were relatively common within the population. This rattle in the shape of a gourd or squash may have been a ritual item used in ceremonies related to agriculture or fertility. With its simple style and lack of decoration, this particular piece may have been a child's toy or a commoner's version of a ritual instrument. Squashes were one of the first domesticates of Mesoamerica and provided a rich source of reliable calories for millennia.

Ocarina
Diquis (Costa Rica)
ca. 500-1000 CE
Ceramic
3 1/8 x 3 1/4"
Museum purchase, 65.050.060

Wind instruments like this ocarina were used as a means to ritually connect with beings of the natural world. As ancient Costa Rican society became increasingly populous and organized, shamanistic spirit connection was even more important for the success of extended family clans. This spinning top form of ocarina is painted in a common style known as Buenos Aires polychrome with red and black linear patterning on a cream colored slip.

Ocarina
Diquis (Costa Rica)
ca. 1000-1550 CE
Ceramic
3 ³/₄ x 5 ¹/₂ x 2 ¹/₄"
Gift of Candice Barrs, 94.0014.09

Painted in Buenos Aires style polychrome, this jaguar ocarina is in a form known as Birmani style, with two tilted heads, four legs, and a number of perforations to allow for a variety of notes. Expressions on the faces of the jaguar are festive and non-threatening. Many musical instruments were made in animal effigy form, and the qualities associated with the jaguar, such as strength, cunning, and power, were traits often honored in ritual musical performances.

Necklace
Costa Rica
ca. 300-800 CE
Jade
12 ³/₄ x 2 ¹/₈ x ³/₈"
Gift of Dr. and Mrs. Abraham Rotbart, 97.0039.04

Around the year 700 jade carving virtually disappeared in Costa Rica as metallurgy became the primary artistic medium for ritual and symbolic items. Although gold became the most highly prized ornament, jade still held symbolic importance and it continued to be a revered item found primarily among the ruling classes. This necklace is composed of small, dark green, cylindrical beads, accented by four large square beads and a large celt-style pendant of lighter green. Because greenstone of all colors was so precious, even tiny fragments were worked into delicate beads like these. The artist who created these tiny jade beads surely spent thousands of hours hand drilling and polishing each piece.

Source: Snarskis (2003)

Necklace
Greater Nicoya (Costa Rica)
ca. 1000-1550 CE
Greenstone, jade
10 3/8 x 1 7/8 x 3/8"
Gift of Sylvia Coppersmith in memory of Dora Coppersmith, 86.0061

Stone beads ranging in size and shape set off a large pendant of an abstracted avian axe-god. This power of birds as spirit companions and symbols of life force continued for millennia throughout Mesoamerica, but especially in the Guanacaste-Nicoya region. Greenstone and jade were used interchangeably for decorative items, demonstrating that the significance was in the color and form, not necessarily the geology.

Source: Snarskis (2003)

Male Axe-God Half-Celt
Costa Rica
ca. 300-900 CE
Jade
8 3/4 x 2 1/4 x 3/8"
Gift of The Rubin-Ladd Foundation, 2007.4.15

This half-celt has been sliced off of the original, in keeping with other anthropomorphic jade objects from Costa Rica. It was carved during the peak of Costa Rican jade-carving popularity and is in the form of a male axe-god deity. The upper part of the celt is carved in the form of a human or deity body with up raised arms, an open mouth, and an extended tongue. The deity wears a large headdress and the head itself is set off from the rest of the celt by side notches. Many shamanic images in Costa Rican art include hands resting on the belly, which may be a reference to fertility. Jade's color and reflective properties provided a symbolic representation of water, a basic resource controlled by each chiefdom. The celt—thought to originate as a tool for woodworking or agriculture but here elevated to a luxury status indicator—provides additional evidence of the importance of man's cooperation with the natural world.

Source: Snarskis (2003), Stone (2002)

Avian Pendant
Greater Nicoya (Costa Rica)
ca. 300-800 CE
Jade
4 1/8 x 7/8 x 1/2"
Gift of Seymour Rosenberg, 72.016.052

Jade carving was likely introduced to the ancient people of Costa Rica by the Olmec. This pendant is modeled after the lovely *quetzal* bird *(Pharomachrus mocinno)*, one of the most dramatic and beautiful birds of the American tropics. The brilliant, iridescent green plumage of the quetzal is symbolized by the reflective, deep green color of the jade stone. Although highly abstracted, the characteristic tuft of feathers on the head of a quetzal is clearly indicated. Birds, and especially quetzals, were especially admired throughout ancient Mesoamerica for their brilliant tail feathers that floated behind them. It is likely that pendants such as this one were talismans that connected a person of importance with their avian animal companion spirit.

Source: Snarskis (2003)

Ornament
Diquis (Costa Rica)
ca. 700-1550 CE
Gold
7/8 x 2 x 1 3/4"
Gift of Mr. and Mrs. Barry Fitzmorris, 2007.52.20

Around the beginning of the Common Era, Costa Rica adopted gold and copper metallurgy from the northern highlands of modern Colombia. Metals eventually replaced jade in importance as the medium for ritual and status marking art. Traded among ruling chiefs and other political or religious leaders gold ornaments such as this one were symbols of prestige and rank. Twin jaguars with long curling tails and snarling teeth are mounted on two parallel bars. Additional small gold ornaments dangle from suspension holes and jingle against the jaguar figures, further accentuating the power of the ornament by bringing it to life. This ornament was likely worn by a high ranking chief, and it is one of a very limited number of gold pieces still intact outside of Costa Rica. Because Europeans cherished this material so highly, much of the pre-Columbian gold art they encountered was melted down and sent to Spain.

Source: Esquivel (2008)

Ceremonial Mace Head
Greater Nicoya (Costa Rica)
ca. 1–500 CE
Stone
3 7/8 x 4 1/4 x 5 1/8"
Museum purchase, 88.0008

Ceremonial mace heads were likely status markers that represented hereditary ties or clan membership by affiliation with a powerful animal, human, or geometric form. Like most mace heads, this one does not show signs of use, and it was probably made to accompany the burial of a powerful individual. The jaguar iconography of this piece and the very fine white limestone from which it was made suggest that the owner was seen as strong, cunning, and powerful—the symbolic characteristics most often associated with felines—though it may have been his extended family, that possessed attributes.

Source: *LAM* (1990), Stone (2002)

Ceremonial Mace Head
Greater Nicoya (Costa Rica)
ca. 1–500 CE
Stone
4 x 3 7/8 x 4 7/8"
Museum purchase, 88.0009

Mace heads have been called "art-weapons" and "art-tools" because they channeled symbolic information via a utilitarian form. Very common in high status graves, they are tied to the emergence of a ruling class dependent upon agricultural intensification and territorial land claims. The anthropomorphic face of this object suggests characteristics of both a human and a monkey, and it may represent a shaman in the process of transformation from human to spirit form. It also shows a very strong similarity to the jaguar mace head, which suggests that they were made by the same artist or were part of the same grave. Together, they demonstrate a social transition during this time period, during which a greater reliance upon powerful people determined the prosperity of the group.

Source: *LAM* (1990)

Jar
Greater Nicoya (Costa Rica)
ca. 300-500 CE
Ceramic
12 x 11 3/8 x 8 1/2"
Museum purchase, 91.0001

This early effigy jar of a woman with pronounced breasts and detailed sexual organs is decorated with red slip and engraved patterns similar to those found on clay stamps. These representations are cited as evidence that stamps were, in fact, most likely used to decorate the human body. Skin decoration was common for both men and women and may have been applied during rituals. In ancient Costa Rica, women commonly held ritual roles, such as healers, guardians of sacred objects, or specialized mediators between humans and spiritual forces.

Sources: Esquivel (2006), *LAM* (2006)

Jar
Greater Nicoya (Costa Rica)
ca. 300-500 CE
Ceramic
8 7/8 x 6 x 5 1/4"
Gift of Thea Katzenstein, 97.0005

The important role of women in daily life as well as ritual is evidenced by the numerous examples of effigy jars, such as this one, that depict female figures with ritual decorations. The black slipped jar is incised with a large variety of body markings and other decorations. Some groups also practiced cranial modification as a ritual practice or status indicator, and this ancient form of body enhancement can be seen in the shape of the top of this effigy jar.

Source: Esquivel (2006)

Roller Stamp
Greater Nicoya (Costa Rica)
ca. 1-700 CE
Ceramic
1 1/8'" x 1 1/2"
Gift of Candice Barrs, 94.0014.23

Throughout ancient Mesoamerica ceramic stamps were used to decorate cloth, clay, and especially human skin. This roller stamp with a wavy design could have been used to create ink or pigment based body decorations seen on ceramic figurines from this region. Using red pigment from the *annatto* fruit and black pigment from the *guaitil* fruit, mixed with grease or other adhesive, the colors could have been rolled onto the body in preparation for ritual or to indicate group or clan identity.

Source: Esquivel (2008)

Flat Stamp
Greater Nicoya (Costa Rica)
ca. 1-700 CE
Ceramic
1 3/8" x 1 3/4"
Gift of Candice Barrs, 94.0014.25

Both cylindrical and flat stamps were made in the Greater Nicoya area, but flat stamps are more common in its Central region. Both types of stamps were created by hand, and design elements were cut when the material was still soft using a technique called excision which provides high and low relief design. This flat stamp has a geometric design that may represent an abstract jaguar spot or, perhaps, a floral image. It would have been suitable for body decoration or stamping cloth and clay. Little is known about the meaning of these designs or how the stamps were used.

Source: Esquivel (2008), Stone (2002)

Trophy Head
Central Highlands/Atlantic Watershed (Costa Rica)
ca. 1000-1550 CE
Basalt
6 3/4 x 5 x 6"
Gift of Mr. and Mrs. Barry Fitzmorris, 2004.53.8

The Atlantic Watershed area is known for stunning stonework and this carved head is a stone representation of a ritual practice known as the "cult of the trophy head." This was a custom in which prisoners were sacrificially decapitated in rituals to ensure the fertility of the ruling group's lands. Carved as a head and neck only, this freestanding object was meant to be displayed in the burial goods of a powerful chief. Unique hair styles rather than facial features distinguish each trophy head, muted to signify the powerlessness of the dead.

Sources: Esquivel (2006), Stone (2002)

Throne
Central Highlands/Atlantic Watershed (Costa Rica)
ca. 1000-1550 CE
Basalt
14 1/8 x 15 x 7 1/2"
Gift of Jack Sams, 76.034.010

Carved stone thrones for rulers or leaders are found throughout Costa Rica and the Caribbean. Elevation of important individuals relates to shamanic practice and the mounting of various animals to travel into spirit worlds. This particular piece has a bird, human, and jaguar motif carved into the solid sides of the sturdy throne. As in the rest of ancient Mesoamerica, the jaguar is once again used as a symbol of political or spiritual authority. Other carved thrones from the site of Papagayo also have animal imagery, and the combination of bird, human, and jaguar suggests the ability of this leader to transcend the three realms of humans, forest, and sky. Status objects became increasingly important in the later periods prior to European contact.

Source: Stone (2002)

Figure
Diquis (Costa Rica)
ca. 800-1550 CE
Basalt
10 3/8 x 8 x 3 1/4"
Gift of David Trout, 75.024.001

Of ambiguous gender, this rather large stone figure is a good example of an artifact unique to the Costa Rican Diquis zone. Known as peg-based sculptures for the extensions below the feet or grip stones, these solid carved figures may have been tomb markers. In this piece the torso and arms are of the same width, and the artist has gone to great effort to open up the solid piece of basalt in order to differentiate these body parts. The costume and facial expressions are typical for this style of figure where bared teeth and baggy eyes may indicate an elder shaman in the midst of a hallucinogenic trance.

Source: Stone (2002)

Jar
Greater Nicoya (Costa Rica)
ca. 1000-1550 CE
Ceramic
5 1/5 x 7 x 6 1/2"
Gift of Beatrice Drimmer, 94.0064.63

This double spout jar is an example of a distinctive ceramic style known as Murillo appliqué, which is characterized by red, glossy pottery with modeled decorative features. Relatively uncommon, this style was likely influenced by ceramic traditions of South America. Four highly detailed crocodiles and frogs decorate this delicate vessel. These tropical animals were common decorative motifs in the art of Costa Rica and crocodiles in particular appeared often to shamans in visions.

Sources: Day (1982), Stone (2002)

Medicine Jar
Central Highlands/Atlantic Watershed (Costa Rica)
ca. 1000-1550 CE
Ceramic
3 5/8 x 2 7/8 x 2 3/4"
Gift of the Estate of Ann M. Grimshawe, 2001.10.25

By the later periods, trade between regions was common and included such perishable items as woodwork, feathers, and hallucinogenic drugs used in shamanic practices. This medicine bowl likely belonged to a chief or shaman and held such a substance. Quite small, it is decorated in red slip, inscribing, and appliqué jaguar figures. The symbolism of the jaguar motif—commonly used to represent power and strength—indicates that this vessel probably held some sort of strong, powerful substance used for healing or ritual.

Female Figure Holding a Baby
Diquis (Costa Rica)
ca. 1-300 CE
Ceramic
3 1/8 x 2 3/4 x 1 1/2"
Gift of Benedict Rucker, 2002.21.6

This figure of a woman holding a nursing baby is modestly decorated with a black and red linear pattern intended to represent garments, jewelry, and/or decorated skin. Part of a class of figurines that show seated women with children within the Fugitive Red Ware tradition, these objects have a perforation at the neck for suspension. The tradition shows signs of contact with later Chiriqui ceramics, and clearly emphasizes the social importance of reproduction and childcare.

Source: Esquivel (2006), Stone (1977)

Monkey Figure
Costa Rica
ca. 1000-1550 CE
Marble
5 3/4 x 2 1/2 x 5 3/8"
Gift of Enrico Varisco in memory of Roberto Varisco, 2003.63.9

Monkeys are ubiquitous in the art of ancient Mesoamerica, and many of the cultures of the region recognized the monkey's intelligence and capability for learning. Monkeys appear in creation myths and were commonly linked with art, artists, writing, and sexuality. This unusual figurine is made of marble, a material found throughout the mountain ranges of Mesoamerica. Sitting quietly, it has a thoughtful and patient expression. The open design of this piece shows connections to stone carving traditions further south.

Sources: Ferrero (1987)

Jar
Greater Nicoya (Costa Rica)
ca. 1000-1550
Ceramic
6 x 8 1/2 x 6 1/2"
Gift of Mr. and Mrs. Robert M. Bischoff, 84.0255.05

An example of the Jicote Polychrome style, this vessel is shaped like a shoe in order to provide more horizontal surface for decoration while still retaining the liquid inside. Intertwined bands around the rim may represent twin serpents, and the painted design below is certainly a supernatural face. When filled with drink, this vessel must have been placed in soft sand or held as the globular base does not allow it to balance on its own.

Tripod Bowl
Greater Nicoya (Costa Rica)
ca. 1000-1550
Ceramic
5 3/8 x 9 1/4 x 6 3/8"
Gift of Sylvia Coppersmith in memory of Dora Coppersmith, 86.0076

Respect and reverence for the jaguar and its relationship with humans is the focus of this exhibition, and this bowl celebrates this theme. The bowl provides the body of the jaguar, with a modeled head attached to the front and three legs rather than four. Black, cream and red paint were used against an orange background. The artist carefully placed dots and spirals around the rim to accentuate the jaguar's distinctive spots. A bowl of this size and design would have been used for ceremonial feasting.

Incense Burner
Central Highlands/Atlantic Watershed (Costa Rica)
ca. 1000-1550 CE
Ceramic
2 x 8 1/2 x 5"
Gift of Seymour Rosenberg, 72.016.008

Ceramic vessels brought to the Intermediate Area by Maya traders likely influenced this frying pan-shaped incense burner. As the popularity of this form increased, it slowly replaced the more common tripod-style incense burners. A shallow pan is attached to a curving handle with a small animal head decoration. The artists who formed the hollow handle left small balls of clay inside to produce sound when the piece moved. The anthropomorphic appliqué on the handle may give some indication of the ritual importance of this item, and given the absence of burning on the interior, it is likely this object was made in order to be deposited as a tomb or burial offering.

Source: Day (1990)

Tripod Jar
Central Highlands/Atlantic Watershed (Costa Rica)
ca. 1-500 CE
Ceramic
6 1/8 x 5 7/8 x 5 7/8"
Gift of Candice Barrs, 94.0014.27

Tripod jars were made throughout ancient Mesoamerica and may have been based upon the typical domestic hearth of three stones with a central cooking pot. In Costa Rica, especially within the Atlantic Watershed region, artists explored the limits of their medium by stretching the legs of the tripod and adding modeled decorations. This tripod jar in the Ticaban style has an owl added to each hollow leg and small pellets of clay rattle inside. A shell was used while the clay was wet to add rows of small dots to the legs. Being nocturnal animals, owls symbolized darkness, death, and destruction, but they also represented wisdom for their ability to be successful in the threatening nighttime environment.

Sources: Day (1990), *LAM* (2006)

Jar
Greater Nicoya (Costa Rica)
ca. 1000-1550 CE
Ceramic
9 3/8 x 9 1/4"
Gift of Seymour Rosenberg, 72.016.005

This large red-slipped jar has a globular body with a compressed neck and round bottom made to sit in sand or atop another vessel. The upper surface is decorated with a simple floral design. It may have been a jar for daily or secular use rather than for ritual practices, and the tightly restricted neck indicates it must have been used for the transport of water or some other liquid.

Source: Day (1982)

Tripod Jar
Central Highlands/Atlantic Watershed (Costa Rica)
ca. 400-700 CE
Ceramic
11 3/8 x 10 1/2 x 8 1/2"
Gift of The Institute of Maya Studies, 80.0040

Thought to be an incense or offertory burners, this delicate tripod jar is a strong example of the Africa style. The style is characterized by modeled decorations perched above the legs which taper to a fine point and are hollow rattles. The appliqués on this jar are vultures and trophy heads, and the vultures are likely representative of Sibo, the King Vulture, who was an important mythological figure associated with creation and fertility. The trophy heads represent offerings to Sibo, and cutting off the heads of prisoners as fertility offerings was a common ritual practice. Each of the bird decorations is slightly different and this gives the vessel a fascinating narrative appearance.

Sources: Day (1990), *LAM* (2006)

Tripod Jar
Central Highlands/Atlantic Watershed (Costa Rica)
ca. 500-1000 CE
Ceramic
9 3/8 x 7 5/8 x 6 1/2"
Gift of C. Clay Aldridge, 2003.51.44

This tripod jar is also a strong example of the Africa style, with long hollow supports and anthropomorphic decorations. Perhaps a better explanation of this unique form than the suggestion that tripod jars were incense burners is the hypothesis that they were vessels for holding *chicha*, a thick fermented brew. Drinking *chicha* was common during the rowdy, drunken feasts known as *chichadas* that celebrated the life of the deceased during funerary rituals. The figures on this black and highly burnished vessel wear wide brimmed hats and appear to have their hands clasped together as though giving thanks.

Sources: *LAM* (2006), Day (1990)

Jar
Greater Nicoya (Costa Rica)
ca. 1000-1350 CE
Ceramic
10 ½ x 11 x 11 ¼"
Gift of C. Clay Aldridge, 2003.51.60

This jar is an example of Jicote polychrome of the Mascara variety. Jicote is characterized by a large globular body with a compressed neck, flared rim, and simple round bottom. The feline face is specifically characteristic of the Mascara variety of Jicote polychrome. Faces on these vessels are portrayed with two types of eyes and this example shows the slanted teardrop shape surrounding the solid inner pupil. A form of effigy vessel, paint is very effectively utilized on this large jar to convey the sober face of a jaguar or other large feline. A large jar with restricted opening such as this must have been utilized for storage of water or some other important liquid.

Source: Day (1982)

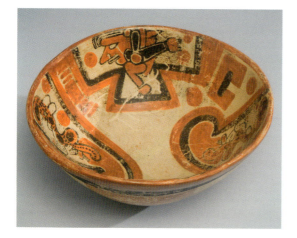

Bowl
Greater Nicoya (Costa Rica)
ca. 1-500 CE
Ceramic
3 ¾ h. x 9"
Gift of Seymour Rosenberg, 72.016.020

Although the term Intermediate Zone has been criticized for an under appreciation of the innovation present in Costa Rican ceramics, it does capture the geographical reality that ideas traveled south from the stratified state societies of central Mexico. In this vibrant bowl, painted in red, black and cream colored slip, we can see a style of depiction that owes much to the ceramic traditions of Oaxaca and the Valley of Mexico. Two humans and two supernatural entities are shown inside cartouches in a very symmetrical arrangement. A masterwork such as this bowl was most likely used by a chief to impress his peers at the competitive feasts that characterized political interactions of ancient Costa Rica.

Tripod Bowl
Greater Nicoya (Costa Rica)
ca. 1000-1550 CE
Ceramic
4 1/2 x 7 1/4 x 8 1/8"
Gift of Seymour Rosenberg, 72.016.014

This tripod bowl was found in Guanacaste although it was most likely made in the Rivas area of modern Nicaragua. During ancient times these modern political boundaries were nonexistent and this area was part of the same cultural sphere. A feline head surrounded by feathers appears on one side with a tail and bird head on the reverse. The legs of the feline rest on two of the leg supports. A feathered jaguar recalls the feathered coyotes and feathered serpents of central Mexican art, although supernatural creatures with overlapping attributes of multiple animals are common throughout the ancient Americas. The combination of modeling and paint, especially a blue pigment, is elaborate and characteristic of Vallejo-type polychromes. The blue paint required an additional, lower temperature firing making these vessels more time intensive than most.

Source: Day (1982)

Tripod Jar
Greater Nicoya (Costa Rica)
ca. 1000-1550 CE
Ceramic
10 x 11"
Gift of Seymour Rosenberg, 81.0234

This tripod jar shows a blend of two common ceramic types. The form is most closely related to the Carmen variety of Pataky polychrome, while the decorative pattern most closely resembles La Maderia polychrome. This jar has a large ovoid shape with a slightly flaring neck and hollow tripod supports. It is painted with typical La Maderia decorative elements, characterized by the black rim with orange bands below and rectangular design panels on the tripod legs. This piece has a guilloche pattern around the rim, a design found throughout ancient Mesoamerica. It usually represents intertwined serpents, such as Quetzalcoatl.

Source: Day (1982)

Jar
Greater Nicoya (Costa Rica)
ca. 1000-1350
Ceramic
10 ¼ x 11 ⅜ x 11 ½"
Gift of Seymour Rosenberg, 81.0235

This large water jar is a more elaborate version of the other Jicote Polychrome jar painted with a jaguar face included in this exhibition. It also has the large globular body, restricted neck and flaring rim. In this example the diagnostic feline face has been painted on the vessel in red and black and a modeled feline head has been added for emphasis. The entire upper surface is covered in swirling geometric designs in red. A vessel this elaborate was certainly used by a high ranking chief, perhaps as a container for the fermented drink *chicha* that was shared at clan feasts.

Bowl
Chiriquí (Panama)
ca. 800-1200 CE
Ceramic
4 ½ x 5 ⅜"
Gift of Greta Gurr, 90.0126.27

Western Panama and southeastern Costa Rica shared a cultural tradition in the ancient past known as Chiriquí. This bowl is likely from a Panamanian site near Barriles, an area where recent archaeological studies have discovered similar artifacts. The pottery from this area is characterized by simple unpainted forms, which include engraved or modeled decoration known as Tarragó Biscuit. The appliqué that decorates this small bowl is exquisitely detailed and shows an anthropomorphic figure holding his head in his hands. There is great emotion in the expression on his face.

Source: Shelton (1995)

Ceremonial Table
Chiriqui (Panama)
ca. 800-1550 CE
Volcanic stone
4 7/8 x 10 7/8 x 6 7/8"
Gift of Greta Gurr, 90.0126.85

This piece, made of volcanic stone, may have served a purpose similar to the ceremonial metates seen in Costa Rica. Used for ceremonial rituals or as thrones for the most powerful rulers to indicate their elevated status, these items were common in the Intermediate area. The decoration on this particular table includes two crocodiles who form the base between two feline heads on either side. The use of these powerful animal symbols, as well as the volcanic stone, supports the notion that this piece was likely part of the grave goods of a powerful ruler.

Source: Shelton (1995)

Tripod Bowl
Chiriqui (Panama)
ca. 1-700 CE
Ceramic
5 1/4 x 5 1/4 x 4 3/4"
Gift of Greta Gurr, 90.0126.69

The Chiriqui were a cultural group whose territory extended into the Diquis Zone of Costa Rica. Many artistic styles were shared throughout this region. This simple tripod bowl, with modeled figures for the legs, is in a style that was typical of Costa Rican pottery, but may have been traded into Panama or imitated by local artists. Three anthropomorphic figures with long ears and goggle eyes decorate the supports of this vase.

Source: Shelton (1995)

Plate
Coclé (Panama)
ca. 600-1000 CE
Ceramic
1 5/8 x 7 1/8"
Museum purchase, 89.0081

Panamanian Coclé ceramics are highly distinctive and reflect a close association between ancient coastal cultures and the fantastic creatures of the sea. This stunning plate depicts a crab in vivid orange, purple and black against a cream-colored background. Dynamic due to the contrasting colors and dramatic black outlines, this bowl is an excellent example of the lively design innovations of Coclé. Thankfully this piece was not smashed in antiquity, as were many elaborate Coclé ceramics interred in wealthy burials.

Source: Stone (2002)

Footed Bowl
Coclé (Herrera Province, Panama)
ca. 600-1000 CE
Ceramic
6 1/2 x 11 1/2"
Gift of an Anonymous Donor, 93.0043.01

The linear patterning of this bowl is typical of the Coclé culture, as is the cream-colored base with red and grey/blue accents. The creatures in each of the four quadrants are variations on a supernatural serpent found very often in Panamanian ceramic art. The footed support is not frequently seen, though during this time period pedestal dishes were common which suggests that this type of support was a variation on the pedestal style.

Source: Helms (1995)

Pedestal Dish
Coclé (Panama)
ca. 600-1000 CE
Ceramic
7 5/8 x 9 1/4"
Gift of Mr. and Mrs. Robert Stoetzer, 89.0082

Pedestal dishes have been described as inspired by the hallucinogenic mushrooms of the tropical lowlands of Mesoamerica, where a variety of fungi were utilized in shamanic rituals. This orange slipped dish is decorated in red and black paint with a fish-serpent image that fills the available interior space. Antennae suggest a catfish is portrayed, an abundant food from the rivers and estuaries of Panama. Red paint was used to signify the life force of this creature.

Sources: Helms (1995)

Feline
Chiriquí (Panama)
ca. 800-1500 CE
Volcanic stone
3 ½ x 8 x 2 ¾"
Gift of Greta Gurr, 90.0126.76

This region of Panama is well known for the Baru Volcano. It has been a major geological feature throughout history and pre-history, with several major eruptions during the Common Era. Volcanic activity produces stone that may have been associated with great power, due to the geological effects associated with seismic activity and eruptions. The importance of felines may be mirrored in the artist's choice of volcanic stone as the medium for this effigy figure.

Source: Shelton (1995)

Staff

BRIAN A. DURSUM, *Director and Chief Curator*

DENISE GERSON, *Associate Director*

KARA SCHNEIDERMAN, *Assistant Director for Collection and Exhibition Services*

JODI SYPHER, *Curator of Education*

HOPE TORRENTS, *School Programs Coordinator*

ADRIANA VERDEJA, *Director of Development*

KERRIE KOSLOWE, *Office Manager*

GITA SHONEK, *Marketing and Communications Assistant*

ALBERTO HERNANDEZ, *Gallery Manager*

MARTIN CASUSO, *Senior Preparator*

DARREN PRICE, *Preparator*

JULIE BERLIN, *Registration Assistant*

LORRIE STASSUN, *Museum Store Manager*

IRENE BERGMANN, *Special Events Coordinator*

YINA BALAREZO, *Membership Coordinator*

JANIE GRAULICH, *Receptionist*

MARIE MILHOMME, *Chief Security Officer*

References

ALCINA FRANCH, JOSE, M. LEON-PORTILLA, E. MATOS MOCTEZUMA
1992   *Azteca Mexica.* Barcelona: Lunwerg Editores.

BAQUEDANO, ELIZABETH
1984   *Aztec Sculpture.* London: British Museum Publications Ltd.

BERRIN, KATHLEEN AND ESTHER PASZTORY
1994   *Teotihuacan: Art from the City of the Gods.* New York: Thames and Hudson.

BOONE, ELIZABETH HILL
2007   *Cycles of Time and Meaning in the Mexican Books of Fate.* Austin: University of Texas Press.

BRUMFIEL, ELIZABETH M.
2008   "Aztec Women: Capable Partners and Cosmic Enemies" In *The Aztec World,* Elizabeth Brumfiel and Gary M. Feinman, eds. Pp: 87-104. New York: Harry N. Abrams.

CARLSON, JOHN B.
2007   Maya Flask Entries. In *The Jay I. Kislak Collection at the Library of Congress.* Washington D.C.: Library of Congress.

CARRASCO, DAVID AND EDUARDO MATOS MOCTEZUMA
2003   *Moctezuma's Mexico: Visions of the Aztec World.* Boulder, Co: University Press of Colorado.

CASO, ALFONSO AND IGNACIO BERNAL
1952   *Urnas de Oaxaca.* Mexico: Instituto Nacional de Antropología e Historia.

COE, MICHAEL, AND JUSTIN KERR
1998   *The Art of the Maya Scribe.* London: Harry N. Abrams.

DAY, JANE S.
1982   Decorated Ceramic Types from the Late Polychrome Period: 1200-1550 A.D. Hacienda Tempisque, Guanacaste Province, Costa Rica. *Vinculos: Revista de Antropología del Museo Nacional de Costa Rica,* Vol. 8, Nos. 1-2: 39-64.

1990   Ritual Art of Pre-Columbian Costa Rica. In *Before Discovery: Artistic Development in the Americas Before the Arrival of Columbus.* Coral Gables: Lowe Art Museum, University of Miami, pp. 62-65.

ESQUIVEL, PATRICIA F.
2006   *Mujeres de Arcilla.* San Jose, Costa Rica: Fundación Museos Banco Central de Costa Rica.

2008   *Sellos precolombinos: Imagenes estampadas de Costa Rica.* San Jose, Costa Rica: Fundación Museos Banco Central de Costa Rica.

EVANS, SUSAN TOBY
2008   *Ancient Mexico and Central America: Archaeology and Culture History.* New York: Thames and Hudson.

FERRERO, LUIS
1987   *Costa Rica Precolumbina: Arqueologia, Etnologia, Technologia, Arte.* San Jose: Editorial Costa Rica.

FURST, PETER T.
1981   "Jaguar Baby or Toad Mother: A New Look at an Old Problem in Olmec Iconography." In *The Olmec and their Neighbors: Essays in Memory of Mathew W. Stirling.* Elizabeth P. Benson, ed. Pp: 149-162. Washington D.C.: Dumbarton Oaks.

GARCIA BARRIOS, ANA
2006   "Confrontation Scenes on Codex-Style Pottery: An Iconographic Review." *Latin American Indian Literatures Journal* 22(2):129-152.

GOLDSTEIN, MARILYN M.
1987   *Ceremonial Sculpture of Ancient Veracruz.* Brookville, N.Y.: Hillwood Art Gallery, Long Island University.

HEALY, PAUL F.
1984   "The Archaeology of Honduras." In *The Archaeology of Lower Central America*, F.W. Lange and D. Stone, eds. Pp:113-164. Albuquerque: University of New Mexico Press.

HELMS, MARY W.
1995   *Creations of the Rainbow Serpent: Polychrome Ceramic Designs from Ancient Panama.* Albuquerque: University of New Mexico Press.

HELMKE, CHRISTOPHE G.B.
2006   "Recent Investigations into Ancient Maya Domestic and Ritual Activities at Pook's Hill, Belize." Papers from the Institute of Archaeology, Vol 17. London: UCL Institute of Archaeology.

KAN, MICHAEL
1970   "The Pre-Columbian Art of Western Mexico: Nayarit, Jalisco, Colima." In *Sculpture of Ancient West Mexico*, Pp: 9-16. Los Angeles: Los Angeles County Museum of Art.

KUBLER, GEORGE
1986   *Pre-Columbian Art of Mexico and Central America.* New Haven: Yale University Art Gallery.

1993   *The Art and Architecture of Ancient America: the Mexican, Maya, and Andean Peoples.* New Haven: Yale University Press.

LINARES, OLGA F.
1977   *Ecology and the Arts in Ancient Panama: on the Development of Social Rank and Symbolism in the Central Provinces.* Washington D.C.: Dumbarton Oaks.

LOWE ART MUSEUM
1990   *Before Discovery.* Coral Gables: Lowe Art Museum, University of Miami.

2003   *Visions of Empire: Picturing the Conquest in Colonial Mexico.* Coral Gables: Lowe Art Museum, University of Miami.

2006   *Lowe Art Museum: Selected Works, Handbook of the Permanent Collection.* Coral Gables: Lowe Art Museum, University of Miami.

LUKE, CHRISTINA MARIE
2002   *Ulua Style Marble Vases.* PhD Dissertation, Cornell University, manuscript on file, Lowe Art Museum.

MARCUS, JOYCE; FLANNERY, KV
1996   *Zapotec Civilization: How Urban Society Evolved in Mexico's Oaxaca Valley.* New York: Thames and Hudson.

MARTIN, SIMON AND NIKOLAI GRUBE
2008   *Chronicle of the Maya Kings and Queens.* 2nd ed. New York: Thames and Hudson.

MATOS MOCTEZUMA, EDUARDO
1988   *The Great Temple of the Aztecs: Treasures of Tenochtitlan.* New York: Thames and Hudson.

MATOS MOCTEZUMA, EDUARDO
2003   *Dioses del México Antiguo.* Mexico: Editorial Océano.

MILLER, MARY ELLEN
2001,06 *The Art of Mesoamerica: from Olmec to Aztec.* New York: Thames and Hudson.

NICHOLSON, HENRY B.
1983   *Art of Aztec Mexico: Treasures of Tenochtitlan.* Washington D.C.: National Gallery of Art.

PASZTORY, ESTHER
1983   *Aztec Art.* New York: Harry N. Abrams.

PRINCETON UNIVERSITY ART MUSEUM
1995   *The Olmec World: Ritual and Rulership.* Princeton, NJ: Princeton University.

RABINOWITZ, ALAN
2000   *Jaguar: One Man's Struggle to Establish the World's First Jaguar Preserve.* Washington D.C.: Island Press.

REENTS-BUDET, DORIE
1994   *Painting the Maya Universe: Royal Ceramics of the Classic Period.* Chapel Hill: Duke University Press.

REYNA ROBLES, ROSA MA.
2003   "La Cultura Arqueológica Mezcala" In *La Cultura Mezcala y el Templo Mayor.* Mexico: Consejo Nacional para la Cultura y las Artes, INAH.

REYNOLDS, RICHARD D.
1993   *The Ancient Art of Colima, Mexico.* Walnut Creek, Ca.: Squibob Press.

SAHAGÚN, BERNARDINO FR.
1992   *Historia General de las Cosas de Nueva España.* Mexico: Editorial Porrúa.

SELLEN, ADAM T.
2005   Catalogue of Zapotec Effigy Vessels. Online publication accessible at www.famsi.org.

SHELTON, CATHERINE N.
1995   A recent perspective from Chiriqui, Panama. *Vinculos: Revista de Antropología del Museo Nacional de Costa Rica*, 20 (1994): 79-101.

SNARSKIS, MICHAEL J.
2003   From Jade to Gold in Costa Rica: How, Why, and When. In *Gold and Power in Ancient Costa Rica, Panama, and Colombia*, Jeffrey Quilter and John W. Hoopes, eds. Pp: 159-204. Washington D.C.: Dumbarton Oaks.

SNARSKIS, MICHAEL J. AND AIDA BLANCO
1978   Dato sobre Ceramica Policromada Guanacasteca Excavada en la Meseta Central. *Vinculos: Revista de Costa Rica.* Vol. 4, No. 2: 106-113.

SOLÍS, FELIPE
2003   "El Hombre Frente a la Naturaleza Mítica" In *Dioses del México Antiguo*, E. Matos Moctezuma, ed. Pp.: 91-99. México: Editorial Océano.

STAIKIDIS, KRYSSI
2006   Where Lived Experiences Reside in Art Education: A Painting and Pedagogical Collaboration with Paula Nicho Cúmez. *Visual Culture and Gender* 1:45-62.

STONE, DORIS
1977   *Pre-Columbian Man in Costa Rica.* Cambridge: Peabody Museum Press.

STONE, REBECCA
2002   *Seeing With New Eyes: Highlights of the Michael C. Carlos Museum Collection of Art of the Ancient Americas.* Atlanta: Michael C. Carlos Museum, Emory University.

TATE, CAROLYN
1995   "Art in Olmec Culture." In *The Olmec World: Ritual and Rulership.* Princeton, NJ: The Princeton University Art Museum.

TAUBE, KARL A.
1988   *The Albers Collection of Pre-Columbian Art.* New York: Hudson Hills Press

1989   Ritual Humor in Classic Maya Religion. In *Word and Image in Maya Culture,* William F. Hanks and Don S. Rice, eds. Pp. 351-382. Salt Lake City: University of Utah Press.

1992   *The Major Gods of Ancient Yucatan.* Studies in Pre-Columbian Art and Archaeology, No.32. Washington D.C.: Dumbarton Oaks.

1993   *Aztec and Maya Myths.* Austin: University of Texas Press.

2004   *Olmec Art at Dumbarton Oaks* Washington, D.C.: Dumbarton Oaks.

2009   "At Dawn's Edge: Tulúm, Santa Rita, and Floral Symbolism in the International Style of Late Postclassic Mesoamerica" In *Astronomers, Scribes, and Priests: Intellectual Interchange between the Northern Maya Lowlands and Highland Mexico in the Late Postclassic Period,* Gabrielle Vail and Christine Hernandez, eds. Pp.145-91. Washington D.C.: Dumbarton Oaks.

TOWNSEND, RICHARD F.
2000   *The Aztecs.* New York: Thames and Hudson.

2003   "Figure of a Seated Chieftain." In *Notable Quotations at The Art Institute of Chicago* Art Institute of Chicago Museum Studies, 29(2): 8-9.

WHITECOTTON, JOSEPH W.
1977   *The Zapotecs: Princes, Priests, and Peasants.* Norman: University of Oklahoma Press.

Contributors

TRACI ARDREN is Associate Professor of Anthropology at the University of Miami and Director of the Program in Women's and Gender Studies. She directs excavations at the Classic Maya center of Xuenkal in Mexico.

BRIAN A. DURSUM is Director and Chief Curator of the Lowe Art Museum. He is currently organizing an exhibition that will feature the Japanese Collection at the Lowe Art Museum, University of Miami, for 2012.

JULIE K. WESP is a graduate student in the Department of Anthropology at the University of California, Berkeley and an alumna of the University of Miami. She is pursuing doctoral research on the bioarchaeology of ancient Oaxaca.

GRETEL RODRÍGUEZ is a graduate student in the Department of Art and Art History at the University of Texas, Austin and an alumna of the University of Miami. Her research has focused on the symbolism and iconography of Aztec and Central Mexican art.

ERICA SEFTON is finishing a degree in paralegal studies. She participated in University of Miami excavations at the Costa Rican site of Isla San Lucas and is an alumna.

GABRIELLE VAIL is a Research Scholar and adjunct member of the faculty at New College of Florida and created the online Maya Hieroglyphic Codices Database. She recently published *The New Catalog of Maya Hieroglyphs, Volume 2: The Codical Texts* (University of Oklahoma Press, 2009) with Martha Macri.